Shrubs

Frances Tenenbaum, Series Editor

 HOUGHTON MIFFLIN COMPANY

Boston • New York 1999

Shrubs

Easy Plants for More Beautiful Gardens

Produced by Storey Communications, Inc.
Pownal, Vermont

Library of Congress Cataloging-in-Publication Data is available.
ISBN 0-395-87333-9

Printed in the United States of America

WCT 10 9 8 7 6 5 4 3 2 1

CONTENTS

INTRODUCTION

Shrubs are one of the most versatile elements in a landscape. They are similar to trees in that both are woody perennials and relatively permanent fixtures; in fact, certain species can be trained to tree shapes. Shrubs also fill many of the same roles as perennials, providing foliage and flowers in a wide range of colors, shapes, and textures.

Shrubs amaze with their hardworking habits, including: low, creeping mats or crawling ground covers; globular tufts or rangy spreaders; and arching sprays or thorny barriers. Used in combination, they can fill a landscape with constant, yet ever-changing interest and provide structural elements such as green carpets, backgrounds thick or thin, and divisions between garden beds, activity areas, and entire properties. With such versatility, it is no wonder we find so many shrubs in formal and informal gardens worldwide, always dependably providing framework and ornament.

Selecting a Shrub

Look at any landscape that appears perfectly kept and attractive in every season. If you analyze its appeal, you will likely find that shrubs play a large part in the composition. Professional designers choose plants carefully for their landscape role and compatibility with their site, visual interest in combination with other plants, performance in several seasons, and ease of maintenance. By applying each of these categories to your own selection process, you can build your own satisfying design using the shrub cultivars included in this book.

The Landscape Role

Before you select a shrub, ask yourself what you expect from it. You may be looking for a filler in a simple foundation grouping, low under windows and taller at the corners. You may want to introduce color and variety to an existing garden. Perhaps a garden setting or a distant view needs a framework. Does an isolated perennial bed need to be linked to a larger whole?

Are you looking for a shrub to mark the top of a stairway, screen an unpleasant view, or add pizzazz and fragrance beside an entry? Of the myriad possible roles for a shrub in the landscape, try to zero in on one or more specific purposes in your landscape.

Site Compatibility

Many gardeners are lured into purchasing a plant by its reputation or sheer beauty with little thought about how they will use it. Then one sunny day with trowel and spade in hand, they try to find just the right spot for it to thrive. If the plant is a short-lived annual or perennial, such an approach may work just fine. If the plant is a shrub, success may be more elusive. For a shrub to thrive and endure, its habit and growth requirements must match the conditions at the planting site. To ensure success, look at the planting site before you purchase a shrub and then select a suitable specimen.

"How is that done?" you may ask. Begin with an understanding of your soil. Is it sand, clay, or silt—or a combination of these three basic soil textures? It is difficult to change what you have, but you can change the structure—the way these particles are put together. If you are lucky enough to have a loam soil, one with a well-balanced combination of these textures, you won't need to make any adjustments.

Most soils benefit from organic amendments to improve both water retention and drainage. Compost—lots of it—or other well-aged organic material improves sandy soils and those with a lot of clay. However, you should amend soil only for shrubs that have small root systems. If you plant a shrub in a hole dug into clay and backfill with amended "potting" soil, then the plant roots will be reluctant to move out of the planting hole and into the surrounding ground, possibly resulting in a dwarfing effect on your shrub.

After you plant a shrub, it is easy to begin improving the soil from the top down by spreading compost on the surface. Also, spread a generous layer of organic mulch on the surface and replenish it constantly. It will provide nutrients to beneficial soil microbes and, in limited amounts, to plant roots.

It is also important to know your soil's pH, the measure of the soil's acidity. Use a home soil-testing kit or take samples to your Cooperative Extension

Service (in some states) or a professional testing lab. Ask the lab for an instruction sheet on collecting a soil sample so that your test results will be accurate.

In addition to appraising the soil, analyze the site itself. Stand in your garden where you would like to plant a shrub. Is there shade overhead? In morning or afternoon? Is the shade lightly filtered from deciduous trees, or heavy from conifers or from the north side of a building? Determine the changes in intensity of sun and shade in each season. When you understand exactly what exposure your shrub will have, consider the space itself. Is there room for the mature size of your plant? Do you need a shrub with a different shape than the one you have in mind?

Finally, impose a few rules on your selection: 1) Never buy a shrub that is not cold hardy or adapted to the conditions in your climate; 2) Never plant a shrub that requires more water than your rainfall or irrigation system can supply. Hand watering with a hose rarely provides reliable moisture for a drought-stressed shrub; and 3) Know what the shrub looks like all year long. It is probably in peak condition when you bring it home from the nursery and may look considerably different in other seasons.

Plant Associations

How will the texture and shape of this shrub look with nearby plants? For the best combinations, consider the range of possibilities from broad-leaved evergreens such as mountain laurel, rhododendron, and azalea to needle-leaved conifers such as juniper and yew; from deciduous shrubs with long periods of flowering such as buddleia, loropetalum, and potentilla to those with short, seasonal bursts such as forsythia and flowering quince. Is foliage or flowering more important? What overall effect are you seeking? Do you need vertical growth for height or horizontal branching for width? A twisted sculpture or arching symmetry?

Try to break out of restrictive patterns and introduce something bold and lively if existing plants lack excitement. Try the velvety purple foliage of purple smokebush or variegated leaves of fiveleaf aralia for rich contrast. Opt for the yellow pompons of kerria, the purple spires of chaste tree, or a sea of pink with beautybush if you are looking for impressive masses of color. Consider fiery red enkianthus or burning bush, twiggy green broom, or a cooling cover of bearberry for notable foliage.

Labor-Intensive or Maintenance-Free?

One of the most important things to consider in selecting a shrub is the required maintenance. The maintenance of a particular shrub depends in part on its nature and in part on what you do to it. Some species, such as forsythia and glossy abelia, are vigorous growers and need regular attention. Others, such as Siberian carpet cypress and heavenly bamboo, never need trimming of any kind and continue to present a perfect picture for years on end. Shrubs that are pruned into formal shapes or hedges require more upkeep, regardless of species, than shrubs planted in informal hedges or naturalistic settings.

The amount of time and energy that you want to devote to garden upkeep should be a key factor in your choice of shrubs. The safest and easiest approach—and most critical for the life of your plants—is to select a shrub that is naturally adapted to its growing site, one that is compatible with all environmental factors and neighboring plants, and one that will not grow beyond the limits of your site.

Yearlong Interest

In a grand public garden, there is space for seasonal shows with plants that have one outstanding period of bloom or turn of leaf. In most home gardens, however, space is at a premium and comeliness year-round makes some plants worthier than others. By combining shrubs with different features in different seasons, you can keep interest alive in your landscape twelve months of the year.

With shrubs, foliage stands out as the one factor that fills a garden with visual delights, season after season. Leaves provide bulk to cover the bare bones of winter, fill empty corners, and hide backgrounds. Evergreens, both broad-leaved and coniferous types, are obvious choices for continuous good looks, but they are not the only solution. Mix species with spring or summer bloom with those sporting vibrant autumn color and berries. Don't overlook valuable cold-season features such as colorful bark, berries, and picturesque branching patterns. Winter highlights—such as red dogwood stems, dangling buds on pieris, and early blooms on winter hazel—may turn out to be the brightest spots in your garden.

GLOSSY ABELIA
Abelia x grandiflora

Zones: 6–9

Type: Evergreen in warm regions, deciduous or semi-evergreen in cold areas

Light: Full to part sun

Size: 6–10 ft. tall, 4–6 ft. wide

Uses: Hedge, screen, shrub border, specimen

Interest: Blossoms from spring to frost; colorful fall foliage

Glossy abelia is a trouble-free, versatile shrub that adds beauty and interest to the garden all year long. Trumpet-shaped ¾-inch flowers appear in clusters at the branch tips in colors varying from white to pink. Long months of flowering are followed by purple-tinted foliage that provides fall and winter interest, especially in areas with mild winters. Abelia's copper-colored sepals persist for months after the flowers drop. The shrub is vase-shaped when young but matures quickly into a densely branched, rounded form with long, wispy branches that arch in graceful cascades.

HOW TO GROW

Abelia thrives in the same soils as rhododendrons and needled evergreens. Plant in full sun to part shade in evenly moist, acidic soil, well amended with organic matter. Once established, the plants are drought-tolerant but should be protected from persistent winds. Prune hedge plants anytime and cut out long shoots as they appear on sheared shrubs. Left unpruned, abelias grow into graceful, flowing shrubs with an attractive cascading effect. To encourage new growth, remove the oldest stems from the shrub base every few years in late winter or early spring.

LANDSCAPE USE

Vigorous and durable, glossy abelia makes an excellent specimen plant or screening shrub for planting in masses. The fountainlike branches are striking both in an island group of three or more and standing alone as an addition to a free-form shrub border. Abelia's colorful appearance and rounded form combine nicely with a background of deeper green conifers. In warmer zones where it remains evergreen, it makes a suitable pruned hedge.

Top Choices

Choose compact, low-growing abelias for planting along the foundation or where space is limited in a shrub or mixed border.

- *A.* 'Prostrata' bears white blossoms; it makes a pleasing 2-foot-tall ground cover.

- *A.* 'Sherwood' forms a dense, 3- to 4-foot mound with pinkish white blooms. The smaller leaves have purple tints in wintertime.

Taylor's Tips

A FLOWERING SHRUB BORDER

For that partially shaded section of the yard, plant a shrub border of rhododendrons and abelias. For the best effect, plant the length of the border in alternating groups of three rhododendrons followed by three abelias. This lovely planting will brighten the yard with colorful flowers from spring to fall.

ONE MORE

Abelia 'Edward Goucher' is a beautiful plant that blends well in evergreen shrub borders. It was created at the turn of the century by Edward Goucher, a plant breeder who crossed glossy abelia with Schuman abelia. The resulting hybrid is similar to glossy abelia but more compact, staying under 5 feet tall. The rich evergreen foliage is covered with showy, dark violet-pink flowers from early summer to early fall. Hardy from Zones 6 to 9.

BOTTLEBRUSH BUCKEYE
Aesculus parviflora

Zones: 5–8

Type: Deciduous

Light: Full to part sun

Size: 10–20 ft. tall,
10–15 ft. wide

Uses: Shrub border,
mass planting

Interest: Midsummer
flowers; colorful fall
foliage

Bottlebrush buckeye is a large, dramatic shrub that adds color and texture to sunny or shady gardens and borders. Its bristly, 8- to 12-inch spikes of white flowers rise above palm-shaped, compound leaves, creating a striking scene in midsummer. After flowering in southern regions, light brown, oval seed capsules that are useful in dried arrangements often appear. For a fall finale, the rich, dark green leaves turn bright yellow to shades of yellowish orange.

HOW TO GROW

Plant bottlebrush buckeye in early spring in a moist, well-drained site. This adaptable plant does well in almost any soil, but it thrives in acidic conditions with ample organic matter. After planting, cover the soil within 3 feet of the plant with several inches of compost or other mulch. You can keep the soil moist and provide organic matter by renewing this mulch layer annually.

In a large garden, give bottlebrush buckeye plenty of space to spread. In a small garden, you can control its growth by removing suckers that form at the base or by root-pruning outside the drip line in early spring. Bottlebrush buckeye has a rounded form that seldom requires pruning. Older plants can be rejuvenated by cutting the stems to the ground in fall.

LANDSCAPE USE

This wide-spreading shrub is excellent for massing in woodland shade, yet it thrives equally well in full or part sun. The protruding pink stamens and erect white flowers make a stunning addition to a shrub border in early to midsummer when few other shrubs are blooming. In an exposed position in an open lawn, bottlebrush buckeye becomes an attractive architectural feature with its layers of broad foliage. Use it also in neglected areas as an easy-care, disease-free cover for difficult banks and slopes.

Top Choices

- *A. parviflora* blossoms a week or two later than the species with slightly larger flower clusters and leaves with less fuzzy undersides.

- *A.* 'Rogers' also blossoms later than the species with spectacular 18- to 30-inch-long clusters of upright flowers.

EXTENDING THE FLOWERING SEASON

Planting a companion vine that climbs through a bottlebrush buckeye effectively extends the bloom season of this handsome shrub. Large-flowered clematis clamber easily through the open branches to display their opulent summertime blooms.

To extend the flower show into late summer and fall, choose blue-purple 'Perle d'Azur' or velvety purple 'Royal Velour'.

The rosy carmine flowers of 'Ville de Lyon' bloom from spring to early fall. This heirloom clematis is a perfect climbing partner for *Aesculus parviflora* 'Rogers'.

BEARBERRY

Arctostaphylos uva-ursi

Zones: 3–7

Type: Evergreen

Light: Full to part sun

Size: 6–8 in. tall, up to 15 ft. wide

Uses: Ground cover, rock garden

Interest: Evergreen foliage; red fall berries

Sometimes called kinnikinnick, a Native American name, bearberry makes an excellent low ground cover for banks and rock gardens. It thrives equally well on upland gravelly slopes, in sandy, infertile soil, in warm interior valleys, or near the salt spray of coastal dunes. Bearberry creeps along the ground, rooting as it spreads, and eventually forms a dense green mat. In rocky terrain, the crooked branches with small, shiny leaves and bright red berries hug the surface, forming attractive patterns and often trailing in loose cascades.

HOW TO GROW

Plant container-grown bearberry in spring in acidic soil, setting the plants 2 feet apart. Do not fertilize to enrich the soil; instead add organic matter to heavy soil to provide good drainage. In hot-summer areas, locate this plant under the protection of open-branched trees; provide periodic watering in the absence of summer rains. While waiting for slow-growing bearberry to spread as a ground cover, fill in bare areas between plants with a coarse mulch such as chipped bark, keeping it away from the crowns of plants. Don't be afraid to walk on mature plants; they can take light traffic, which helps maintain good soil contact with creeping stems.

LANDSCAPE USE

Bearberry's creeping roots make this low shrub ideal for holding soil in place and controlling erosion on steep banks. It can serve as a low-maintenance, large-scale ground cover or as a lawn substitute for smaller plots. You can also use bearberry beneath tall trees where it gets ample filtered sun or between native plants and grasses in a sunny, well-drained meadow.

Top Choices

- *A.* 'Radiant' grows 18 inches tall with rounded, medium green leaves and is especially well suited to coastal gardens.

- *A.* 'Massachusetts' forms a dense, flat mat of glossy foliage dotted with clusters of pink flowers in spring.

- *A.* 'Wood's Red' has large, bright red fall berries and deep green leaves that turn to a reddish shade in winter.

VERSATILE ARCTOSTAPHYLOS

Other species of *Arctostaphylos* yield a broad selection of interesting plants adapted to a wide variety of growing conditions and landscape uses.

Their rich, mahogany red bark and beautiful leaves add unexpected beauty to the garden. Two of the best are:

- Manzanita, *A. densiflora* 'Howard McMinn', has deep green leaves on 6-foot stems peppered with pink flowers in late winter to early spring. Zones 8 to 10.

- White-leaf manzanita, *A. viscida*, reaches a height and width of 12 feet and is densely covered with silvery leaves. It is native to hot inland valleys and hills and grows best in those conditions. Zones 8 to 10.

The glossy leaves of bearberry are especially attractive set against the rough stones of a rock garden.

JAPANESE BARBERRY
Berberis thunbergii

Zones: 4–8

Type: Deciduous

Light: Full to part sun

Size: 2–6 ft. tall, 3–6 ft. wide

Uses: Edging, barrier hedge, ground cover, mass planting

Interest: Colorful foliage and berries

Widely grown as a tough barrier hedge, Japanese barberry is one of the best all-around plants for easy care, bright seasonal color, and adaptability. Dainty, golden yellow flowers open from tiny red buds in spring after new leaves appear. Dense, bright green summer foliage completely cloaks the angled, very thorny branches and turns to brilliant blends of orange, scarlet, and tawny purple in autumn. After leaf drop, Japanese barberry's thorny, reddish brown stems are covered with bright red fruits that persist all winter.

HOW TO GROW

Japanese barberry brandishes its broadest spectrum of autumn hues when planted in full sun. In shade, the fall coloring is less pronounced and foliage is more open. This shrub grows best in average, unimproved soil and performs reliably in all but the hottest regions. Irregular growth from arching branches gives Japanese barberry a graceful character that is ruined by severe shearing. Spaced at 4-foot intervals and left unpruned, the plants mature into a flowing, thorny barrier hedge. Prune older stems to the ground every few years to encourage new growth and brighter leaf color. Rejuvenate old plants by cutting them to the ground in fall.

LANDSCAPE USE

Disease-resistant and tolerant of urban pollution, Japanese barberry is one of the most versatile landscape shrubs. It is often used alone or in small groups in rock gardens and along foundations. The exuberant fall foliage highlights mixed shrub borders and hedgerows, while the prickly stems keep out unwanted traffic. The shrubs make an excellent ground cover when planted in masses along exposed, sunny banks.

Top Choices

- *B.* 'Bonanza Gold' is 2 feet tall with vivid yellow-green leaves.

- *B.* 'Crimson Pygmy' is a bright reddish purple and grows slowly, reaching 1½ to 2 feet tall and 3 to 5 feet wide with age.

- *B.* 'Kobold' is compact with lustrous, dark green leaves on mounded plants 2 feet tall.

- *B.* 'Rose Glow' produces rose-colored new growth that matures to violet-red.

BUTTERFLY BUSH

Buddleia davidii

Zones: 5–9

Type: Deciduous to semi-evergreen

Light: Full sun

Size: 6–10 ft. tall, 6–10 ft. wide

Uses: Specimen, shrub border, wildlife garden

Interest: Fragrant summer flowers

Few shrubs are more decorative in the summer garden than butterfly bush. Many kinds of butterflies are attracted to the fragrant flower panicles that cover this shrub from midsummer until frost. The small flowers are tightly packed in showy cone-shaped clusters 4 to 10 inches long that appear at the tips of arching branches that bow and sway in the wind. The narrow leaves are white and lightly fuzzy underneath, giving the foliage a gray-green appearance.

HOW TO GROW

Full sun, well-drained soil, and average to poor fertility are the basic requirements a butterfly bush needs to thrive. This undemanding shrub is tolerant of a wide range of soil and climate conditions and is able to withstand considerable drought once established.

In cold climates, butterfly bush performs like a hardy perennial, dying to the ground each winter and then growing back the following spring. It rapidly becomes a 4- to 6-foot shrub and is in full flower by midsummer. Even in warm climates, where butterfly bush remains partly evergreen, cut back tall stems in fall to within 6 to 10 inches of the ground. This drastic pruning promotes vigorous new growth and prolific flower production. For the most abundant blossoms, deadhead faded panicles. New stems will quickly form along the stem, producing even more flowers.

LANDSCAPE USE

Extend your enjoyment of the activity and color of butterflies in your garden by planting a butterfly bush near a patio or window. It looks good in an island bed, at the back of a perennial border, or set into a mixed shrub border where its legginess is camouflaged.

Top Choices

- B. 'Black Knight' produces strong, vigorous stems and long panicles of sweetly scented, deep purple blossoms.

- B. 'Harlequin' has dark green leaves edged in white and deep reddish purple, fragrant flowers.

- B. 'Pink Delight' bears long panicles of pure pink, sweetly fragrant flowers.

- B. 'Red Plume' produces burgundy red, richly perfumed flowers.

Taylor's Tips

ATTRACTING BUTTERFLIES

To attract butterflies throughout several seasons, plant a variety of nectar plants in addition to butterfly bush in the garden. Include spirea (*Spiraea* spp.), lilac (*Syringa* spp.), and honeysuckle (*Lonicera* spp.). Surround these shrubs with perennials such as red valerian (*Centranthus ruber*), purple coneflower (*Echinacea purpurea*), and valerian (*Valeriana officinalis*).

PRUNE AND PROTECT BUTTERFLY BUSH

Butterfly bush blooms on the current season's growth and so should be pruned in fall. After flowering is complete, cut all branches to 6 to 10 inches from the ground.

In spring, butterfly bush will sprout new shoots from the roots if winter cold damages any aboveground growth. For optimum winter protection, mound soil around the plant base in fall. After the ground freezes, cover with pine boughs or straw mulch until the soil thaws in spring.

ENGLISH BOXWOOD
Buxus sempervirens

Zones: 5–8

Type: Evergreen

Light: Full to part sun

Size: 3–20 ft. tall,
3–20 ft. wide

Uses: Edging, hedge,
foundation planting,
specimen, topiary

Interest: Evergreen
foliage

English boxwood is the tidiest of garden shrubs, with aromatic, glossy green foliage that neatly covers the stems all the way to the ground. It is attractive whether sheared or left unpruned to grow naturally into dome or oval shapes. Valued for its fine-textured foliage, slow-growing boxwood is the plant of choice for topiary, hedges for a formal garden, edging beds and walkways, and for sculpted foundation plantings.

HOW TO GROW

With careful planning, selection, and planting, English boxwood is relatively undemanding and easy to grow. In parts of the South, where troublesome nematodes are difficult to control, this shrub may be impractical. In other areas, good care eliminates most disease and pest problems.

Give your boxwood a strong start at planting time by mixing a tablespoon of superphosphate into the soil at the bottom of the planting hole. Apply a complete fertilizer when plants are dormant—late winter in the South and early spring in the North. To avoid stimulating tender growth, which is subject to damage by early-season cold, never fertilize English boxwood in summer or early fall. Water if summers are dry.

LANDSCAPE USE

Versatile English boxwood accents the landscape in many ways. The plants are excellent specimens when planted near a perennial or herb garden. Low-growing forms make dense formal hedges that add a sophisticated look to any landscape. Left unpruned, English boxwood is ideal for mass plantings, turning slopes or other areas into a sea of glossy, dark green leaves. English boxwood is one of the best plants for topiary and can be crafted into almost any shape.

Top Choices

- *B.* 'Elegantissima' is as elegant as its name implies with deep green leaves touched with white.

- *B.* 'Northern Beauty' is slightly more hardy than the species and much less susceptible to wind and sun damage. Zones 4 to 8.

- *B.* 'Suffruticosa' is a compact, slow-growing form with dense, very glossy foliage.

- *B.* 'Welleri' is low-growing (3 feet tall, 5 feet wide) with deep green winter color.

Taylor's Tips

CONTROLLING BOXWOOD BLIGHT

Boxwood blight is a fungus that attacks healthy twigs and branches of this shrub. It spreads quickly in warm, humid weather, causing the leaves on an entire branch to turn yellow. To control boxwood blight, remove winter-damaged wood and dead leaves in spring. Next, spray the bushes with lime-sulfur fungicide. Keep fungicide away from animals and do not spray plants when the temperature is over 80° F.

WINTER WEATHER

Most English boxwood cultivars need protection from desiccating winds and sunscald. In cold-winter areas, choose the hardiest cultivars and locate plants in sheltered sites out of direct wind and winter sun. The foliage can be damaged in freezing temperatures after being exposed to daytime sunlight. Wherever it's planted, use a layer of mulch and regular watering to help reduce damage by keeping the roots cool and moist. In coastal areas, plant boxwood in full sun.

PURPLE BEAUTYBERRY
Callicarpa dichotoma

Zones: 5–8

Type: Deciduous

Light: Full sun to light shade

Size: 4 ft. tall, 4 ft. wide

Uses: Shrub border, specimen

Interest: Lilac-purple berries in fall

Grown for its magnificent, eye-catching display of colorful fall fruits, purple beautyberry is a favorite shrub for unusual late-season color. The intense, often iridescent lilac berries begin to ripen in late summer and persist into winter. The shiny fruits are clustered along arching stems and contrasts beautifully with red and yellow autumn foliage. Later in the season, purple beauty-berry stands out against a background of snow, giving life to leafless landscapes.

HOW TO GROW
Purple beautyberry likes sunny or lightly shaded, protected sites sheltered from ravaging winds. Soil should be loose and well drained with ample organic matter, but average conditions are adequate. For the best berry production, do not fertilize. Treat purple beautyberry as

you would an herbaceous perennial, cutting it to within 6 inches of the ground in early spring. If plants are killed back by severe cold, remove deadwood in early spring. New shoots will usually resprout from the base in a few weeks.

LANDSCAPE USE

Purple beautyberry produces more berries than other *Callicarpa* species and also has a more attractive, refined form. The long, wispy branches of this shrub arch to the ground, carrying foliage in even layers and giving it appeal before fruits develop. When planted 3 to 4 feet apart in groups, this shrub makes an effective bank of fall color. Beautyberry always attracts attention as a specimen when planted near a drive or entryway where its riveting colors can be seen close up. Include beautyberry in a mixed bed or border with carefully selected blues and violets of late-flowering asters, or set it at the edge of a woodland to pick up interest after spring and summer performers have finished their shows.

Top Choices

- *C. dichotoma* var. *albafructus*, white beautyberry, is similar to the species in size and shape but offers abundant clusters of snow-white berries in fall. It is stunning planted near dark green evergreens.

- *C. bodinieri* var. *giraldii* 'Profusion', Bodinier beautyberry, bears less fruit than purple beautyberry but offers foliage that turns a lovely watercolor shade of rosy violet in fall. Zones 6 to 8.

INVIGORATING BEAUTYBERRIES

Pruning in late winter or early spring stimulates new growth that will bear flowers in summer and fruit in fall. This technique is valuable on plants that flower on wood produced in the current season, but it prevents flowering on those shrubs that bloom on last year's growth.

You can promote spectacular fruiting on beautyberry bushes by pruning last year's stems to the ground. In cold-winter areas, wait until the weather has started to warm in early spring before pruning.

To keep moisture from collecting over the crown, use a sharp pruning tool to make clean cuts at a slight angle away from the center of the shrub. After the soil has warmed, add a layer of organic mulch around the root zone, keeping it 6 to 12 inches away from the base of the plant.

SWEET SHRUB
Calycanthus floridus

Zones: 5–9 and milder parts of Zone 4

Type: Deciduous

Light: Full sun to full shade

Size: 6–9 ft. tall, 6–10 ft. wide

Uses: Foundation planting, shrub border, specimen

Interest: Fragrant summer flowers; colorful fall foliage

Pest- and disease-free, this is one of the best all-around shrubs for general use. Sweet shrub, also called Carolina allspice, is an East Coast native. Its unusual spicy, reddish brown flowers appear in abundance for several weeks in late spring, and sporadically throughout summer and early fall. The gentle aroma of the mature flowers suggests cider or pineapple. Fall color varies from plant to plant, often yellow to gold, but is sometimes absent completely. Leaves persist on the branches until late fall or early winter.

HOW TO GROW
Easy-care sweet shrub adapts to nearly any soil, but it thrives in deep, moist loam that is rich in organic matter. Light shade is needed for the darkest green leaf color and tallest height. Prune lightly by thinning out any crowded

branches and deadwood. To avoid removing the current season's blooms and to control the shape, prune the branch ends after flowering. Cold temperatures in northern latitudes may kill aboveground stems, but sweet shrub will grow back from the roots. To protect against winter conditions, cover the base of the shrub with straw after the ground has completely frozen.

LANDSCAPE USE

Versatile sweet shrub fits into nearly every garden situation. Its clean, glossy foliage harmonizes easily with other shrubs and enlivens any type of border in sun or shade. Its irregular but graceful branching habit fits naturally beneath tall deciduous trees and among rhododendrons, oakleaf hydrangeas, or pieris. Use it also to grace corners of buildings or as a specimen in a lawn.

Enjoy the fruity, spicy fragrance of sweet shrub along a woodland path, beside a bench, or as a privacy screen near a patio. In earlier times, the fragrant flowers were used to freshen linens, and the dried bark was used as a substitute for cinnamon.

Top Choices

- C. 'Edith Wilder' is a rare variety with flowers typical of the species in appearance, but much more fragrant.

- C. 'Purpureus' has maroon-brown flowers and dark green foliage tinted with purple underneath.

- C. 'Urbana' was developed in the Midwest. Its maroon-brown flowers have a slightly sweeter fragrance than the species.

PROPAGATING SWEET SHRUB

Sweet shrub has been grown in gardens since 1726. It has never been an easy plant to propagate, but if the seeds are gathered at the correct time they germinate well.

1 After the flowers have faded, watch for the fruits to begin to develop. In mid- to late summer the urn-shaped fruits begin to change color, turning from green to brown.

2 Slip on a pair of rubber gloves and with pruning shears snip the fruit from the stem. Gently but firmly crush the fruit and look for the greenish-colored seeds. The seed coat should still be soft. Seeds that have hard seed coats will not germinate well.

3 Sow the seeds in a container filled with fine potting soil, setting the seeds just under the soil surface. Cover with a layer of vermiculite and moisten.

CAUTION: Sweet shrub's nutlike brown fruits do not develop every year after flowering. Like the flowers, the fruit is aromatic when crushed, but it is also toxic and causes convulsions if ingested.

CAMELLIA
Camellia japonica

Zones: 8–9 and milder parts of Zone 7

Type: Evergreen

Light: Part shade

Size: 6–15 ft. tall, 6–15 ft. wide

Uses: Bonsai, container plant, foundation planting, espalier, shrub border

Interest: Showy flowers; evergreen foliage

Camellias, with their delicate, waxy flowers and glossy foliage, lend a formal, dignified look to warm-region gardens all year long. The many varieties offer a range of exquisite blossoms, from single to semi-double and double forms in white, pink, or red. Set in a partly shady shrub border or used as an accent in court-yards and patios, camellias provide a deep green back-ground throughout the year. In late fall to spring, the plants are decorated with scentless but stunning flowers. In northern areas, camellias can be grown as container plants and overwintered indoors.

HOW TO GROW

Camellias perform best in sheltered, partly shaded sites in climates with mild winters. Transplant them when the plants are in bloom. Plant container-grown or bareroot plants in acidic soil, amended with peat or compost to improve drainage and conserve soil moisture. Where soil is heavy or water is high in salts, plant in a raised bed. Take care to keep the crown above the soil line. Mulch the shallow roots with a 2-inch layer of bark chips or pine needles. Each year before and immediately after flowering, apply an acidifying fertilizer. Keep the soil evenly moist to reduce bud drop, though this condition can also be caused by sudden temperature changes.

LANDSCAPE USE

The camellia is a naturally attractive plant with an appealing form that needs no pruning except for removing wayward shoots or when grown in specialized habits. Young plants can be trained as espalier (see page 97) or as bonsai but are most commonly used as freestanding entry or accent plants. When planted along foundations or walls, give camellias either a northern or an eastern exposure.

Top Choices

- C. 'Elegans' has dark purple-rose blossoms sometimes streaked with white in the center.

- C. 'Guilio Nuccio' has an abundance of large semidouble, rose-colored flowers on attractive, upright stems.

- C. 'Mrs. D. W. Davis' produces very large, semidouble, blush pink blossoms on compact stems.

- C. 'Purity' bears pure white, double flowers.

CONTROLLING FLOWER BLIGHT

Flower blight is a serious problem from California to the Atlantic coast. The disease organisms live in the soil but only damage the flowers, beginning as small brown specks on the petals that spread until the entire flower is brown. To control flower blight:

1 Inspect all container-grown plants before purchase. Bareroot plants are generally free of the disease.

2 Keep the area around camellias clean, removing fallen flowers and buds regularly.

3 Cover the soil with several inches of fresh compost, pine needles, or bark chips after flowering.

CAMELLIAS IN A WOODLAND GARDEN

Under the high, open canopies of deciduous trees, mix camellias with rhododendrons and azaleas, Virginia sweetspires, variegated aralias, fothergillas, Virginia bluebells, and hardy fuchsias. They also look lovely when combined with evergreen hollies, hostas, and ferns.

BLUE MIST SHRUB

Caryopteris x *clandonensis*

Zones: 6–9 and milder parts of Zone 5

Type: Deciduous

Light: Full sun

Size: 2–3 ft. tall, 2–3 ft. wide

Uses: Rock garden, shrub or perennial border

Interest: Aromatic leaves; late-summer flowers

Blue mist shrub, also known as blue spirea and blue-beard, is one of the best small shrubs for late-summer color. Long a standard in traditional cottage gardens, this low-maintenance shrub also adds soft, hazy blue color to perennial borders. Pale gray-green leaves emerge in spring on elongating stems and by late summer, feathery blue flowers appear in clusters at their tips. In all but the warmest zones, blue mist shrub acts more like a perennial than a shrub, its tender stems dying to the ground in winter.

HOW TO GROW

A little extra care at planting time to give blue mist shrub excellent drainage will pay off with a longer-lived, healthier plant. Improve clay and loose sandy soils by adding ample organic matter. Where soil is heavy and drainage is slow, plant on small mounds or in raised beds to protect the roots from excess winter moisture. Blue mist shrub needs warm summers and full sun to produce the most abundant growth and flowering. Supplemental fertilizers are usually not needed and, when used, can even reduce flowering and cause weak, floppy branches. Prune back all top growth in very early spring, leaving two pairs of buds at the base of each stem. Blooms will appear on the current season's growth.

LANDSCAPE USE

Blue mist shrub is valuable in spring as a low, mounding edging plant around roses and mixed borders. In summer, its small blue flowers blend well with late-blooming roses; in autumn, its cool blues are superb contrasts to yellow and gold daisies, pink roses, or bright crimson kaffir lilies. Include it with low-growing ornamental grasses or tucked among boulders in a sunny rock garden.

Top Choices

- C. 'Blue Mist' bears powder blue flowers with abundant, dark green leaves.

- C. 'Dark Knight' has violet-blue blossoms and dark green leaves.

- C. 'Longwood Blue' has lush, compact growth, silvery foliage, and wands of lavender blue flowers. The abundant blooms also make superb cut flowers.

Taylor's Tips

DECORATING WITH
BLUE MIST SHRUB

The blue flowers of blue mist shrub add a soft balance to the hot yellows, golds, and reds of the late summer garden. Plant blue mist shrub near black-eyed Susans, bright yellow false sunflowers, or brick red 'Autumn Joy' sedums.

BLUE MIST AS A
LOW HEDGE

Plant this fast-growing shrub as an informal seasonal hedge. It can be used as a background hedge to accent low-growing perennials or as a serpentine hedge that weaves through lavenders and lobelias in borders or cottage gardens. At the end of any style hedge, group three or more blue mist shrubs in a mass for a bold look.

FLOWERING QUINCE
Chaenomeles spp.

Zones: 4–8

Type: Deciduous

Light: Full to part sun

Size: 4–8 ft. tall, 4–6 ft. wide

Uses: Wildlife planting, shrub border

Interest: Spring flowers; fall fruits

Flowering quince is grown for the rich vermilion, coral red, delicate pink, or pure white flowers that cover its twiggy stems in late winter or early spring. Other shrubs may surpass it in beauty, but none challenge its nostalgic presence and charming flowers that resemble apple blossoms. In winter, the unadorned, thorny branches take on an interesting, contorted, sculptural form. Reliable in northern climates, flowering quince does not tolerate hot, humid regions south of Zone 8. In such conditions, the plants become stressed and often drop their lower leaves in summer.

HOW TO GROW
Flowering quince adapts to most garden locations with well-drained soil. Mature plants are drought-tolerant but young plants need regular watering. All plants,

regardless of age, benefit from an all-purpose, balanced fertilizer applied annually in late spring after flowering. Full sun promotes best flowering, while shade results in only scattered blooms. Prune annually after blossoming, removing the oldest stems and any unwanted suckers from the base of the plant. If shaping is needed, prune branches back by one-third. To renew old shrubs, cut all growth back to within 6 inches of the ground.

LANDSCAPE USE

The irregular habit of flowering quince makes it a valuable addition to informal plantings and wildlife gardens. Left unpruned, it yields a beautiful floral display. Its thick, twiggy interior provides a useful refuge for birds. In rural areas, its informal shape looks good along roadways and fence lines. Flowering quince is so durable that it often flowers long after gardens have been abandoned.

Top Choices

- *C. japonica* 'Cameo Apricot' bears apricot-pink blossoms.

- *C. speciosa* 'Toyo-Nishiki' is an upright grower with white, pink, and red flowers appearing on the same plant.

- *C. x superba* 'Texas Scarlet' bears crimson blossoms on its compact and spreading stems.

DISPLAYING
FLOWERING QUINCE

One of the best ways to display flowering quince is to train its slender branches into irregular patterns as a wall shrub. Held against a wall, it becomes an upright foliar background useful for highlighting fall-blooming perennials or accenting a climbing vine such as pink *Clematis* 'Dutchess of Albany'.

1 To train, cut off shoots growing toward or away from the wall and cut flowering branches back to two or three buds from the main stem.

2 Tie stems loosely to the wall to maintain shape.

3 Remove suckering growth around the base to preserve a narrow shape. You can replant rooted suckers elsewhere in a hedge or as freestanding plants to provide branches for forced blooms and winter arrangements.

SUMMER-SWEET
Clethra alnifolia

Zones: 5–9

Type: Deciduous

Light: Full to part sun

Size: 9 ft. tall,
6–12 ft. wide

Uses: Shrub border, specimen

Interest: Fragrant summer flowers; colorful fall foliage

Summer-sweet, or sweet pepperbush, blooms in summer in sun or part shade. In an ideal environment of constant moisture and loose, rich soil, it reaches a sturdy 9-foot height, but in average conditions, it usually stays under 6 feet. Summer-sweet is loved for its deliciously fragrant, 4- to 6-inch-long, upright flower spikes in creamy white, pink, or rose. Yellow and golden hues take over for several weeks in fall before leaf drop, which reveals attractive brown fruit capsules that persist through winter.

HOW TO GROW
Native to wetland areas of the East Coast, summer-sweet grows best in acidic soils rich in organic matter. Where conditions are alkaline, the foliage tends to develop chlorotic yellow spots. Keep the surface of sandy soil covered with several inches of compost or other mulch

around the root zone to hold in moisture. If growth is sluggish or flowering is sparse, apply a balanced, all-purpose fertilizer in late winter or early spring.

LANDSCAPE USE

Summer-sweet performs best when it is allowed to naturalize in lightly shaded, moist sites. Plant it near seeps and drainage ditches to take advantage of its ability to colonize wet spots. In ordinary garden sites, remove any suckering growth every year or two to prevent unwanted spreading. Plant five or more summer-sweets 5 to 6 feet apart for a summer-blooming hedge, or to conceal a low fence or other structure.

As a woodland understory shrub, combine summer-sweet with camellias, azaleas, and rhododendrons to follow their spring-time blooms. In a mixed border, partner it with perennials or use it as a support for an early-blooming, climbing clematis. For a summer evening treat, plant summer-sweet near a porch or entry where you can enjoy its sweet and spicy, clovelike scent.

Top Choices

- *C.* 'Hummingbird' is a 3- to 4-foot dwarf that bears large quantities of white flowers.

- C. 'Paniculata' is the most vigorous grower with 6-inch, showy white blooms.

- C. 'Pink Spire' has rosy pink buds and pink blossoms.

- C. 'Rosea' buds are dark pink, opening to pale pink blossoms that fade to blush.

Taylor's Tips

SELECTIVE PRUNING

Summer-sweet develops its most attractive form when left unpruned. After several years, however, the oldest branches may stop flowering. Rejuvenate the bush by removing the oldest branches completely at the base of the shrub; use a long-handled pruner or a pruning saw.

THE OTHER CLETHRA

C. barbinervis, Japanese clethra, grows 12 to 15 feet tall and brings one of the best winter silhouettes to the garden. The smooth gray-brown bark assumes a quiet dignity with age as it sheds curly flakes.

In summer, drooping panicles of lightly fragrant white flowers appear at the tips of the branches. Birds, including sparrows, phoebes, titmice, and chickadees, are attracted to its branches all year long.

RED-OSIER DOGWOOD
Cornus sericea

Zones: 2–7

Type: Deciduous

Light Full sun to full shade

Size: 10 ft. tall, 10 ft. wide

Uses: Mass planting, shrub border, wildlife garden

Interest: Spring flowers; fall foliage and berries; colorful stems in winter

Red-osier dogwood is one of the few ornamental shrubs that bring several seasons of color to the coldest climates. Reliable even in the far North, this dogwood is more tolerant of hot-humid summers than similar Tartarian dogwood (*C. alba*). Best-loved for its winter interest, red-osier dogwood stands out in leafless, cold-weather landscapes. Its vivid red or bright yellow stems bear white flower clusters in spring. In fall, the rich green leaves turn purplish red.

HOW TO GROW

A native of low, wet areas, red-osier dogwood grows vigorously in moist, swampy sites, forming thickets that rise from underground stems. Less invasive in dry sites, it tolerates clay and sandy conditions. For best color, plant red-osier dogwood in full sun. You can keep this shrubby dogwood small by pruning every one to three years. Either cut each stem to the base in spring to generate all-new growth, or cut out only the oldest branches that have lost their brightness. New growth has the most intense color. If twig blight is a problem in your area, annual pruning is an effective control.

LANDSCAPE USE

Wet sites, such as the perimeter of a water garden, are ideal for red-osier dogwood. Planted along a creek bed or pond, its dense, fibrous roots hold soil in place. The glossy winter stems are bold companions for river birch (*Betula nigra*), echoing the reddish tones in its bark. Bright yellow-stemmed varieties combine well with vivid young willows or somber green conifers.

Top Choices

- C. 'Cardinal' changes colors with the seasons—from yellow-green in spring, to red in fall, and then fading to orange in winter.

- C. 'Flaviramea' has glistening yellow stems in winter and is very effective when planted with evergreens.

- C. 'Golden Twig' is a striking and popular yellow-stemmed cultivar.

- C. 'Silver and Gold' has golden stems with cream-edged, variegated foliage that turns plum purple in fall.

OTHER RED-STEMMED DOGWOODS

Tartarian dogwood is a red-stemmed species but does not produce yellow-stemmed varieties as red-osier dogwood does. It is more cold hardy but less vigorous and spreads more slowly.

- 'Spaethii' is an excellent variety with leaves edged in yellow.

- 'Ivory Halo', with variegated foliage, is a compact 2- to 5-foot plant, valued for small spaces.

A DOGWOOD HEDGE

Red-osier and Tartarian dogwoods are useful hedge plants, particularly in northern climates. Set plants 5 to 6 feet apart for a hedgerow that will fill in after a few years. Trim the hedge to the ground for best stem color or thin selectively for greater height.

FRAGRANT WINTER HAZEL

Corylopsis glabrescens

Zones: 5–8

Type: Deciduous

Light: Full sun to part shade

Size: 8–15 ft. tall, 8–15 ft. wide

Uses: Shrub border, woodland garden

Interest: Fragrant late-winter to early-spring flowers; colorful fall foliage

The pale yellow blossoms of fragrant winter hazel are a welcome signal of winter's end. Before leaves bud out, flower clusters dangle in a zigzag arrangement from slender, pale brown branches. For the rest of the year, this broad-spreading shrub is a handsome mound of large leaves that are dark green above and pale beneath. They turn yellow-gold in fall. With selective pruning, fragrant winter hazel can be trained into a multi-stemmed small tree. Although the late-winter or early spring flowering period is brief, this is still one of the best large shrubs for early-season color.

HOW TO GROW

Choose a site in sun or part shade that offers some protection from strong winds and late frosts that can damage the flowers. Fragrant winter hazel grows well in average garden conditions but does best in evenly moist, loose, acidic soil. Where soils are alkaline, mix in peat moss or leaf mold at planting time over an 8- to 10-foot-wide area; then apply a fertilizer designated for camellias or rhododendrons.

LANDSCAPE USE

Fragrant winter hazel is useful as a large, free-flowing shrub at the back of a deep border or at the edge of a woodland. Plant it near a walkway where its cheerful blooms are easily visible and their scent can be most appreciated. The pale flower clusters stand out best when they are displayed against a dark background, such as the leeward side of a wall or a stand of deep green conifers. With its lower branches pruned back, fragrant winter hazel supplies a graceful focal point in a lawn or a mixed bed. Surround it with early-blooming rhododendrons such as brightly colored 'Cornell Pink', crocuses, or Virginia bluebells (*Mertensia virginica*) for a truly colorful early-spring show.

Top Choice

- C. *pauciflora,* buttercup winter hazel, is a dainty shrub growing from 4 to 6 feet tall. In early spring, its brown branches are covered with primrose yellow flowers. The small, cupped blossoms have a light, pleasing fragrance. It is more tolerant of alkaline soils than fragrant winter hazel and does well at the edge of woodlands or in a mixed shrub border. Zones 6 to 8.

FORCING WINTER HAZEL

Thin and shapely winter hazel branches are a favorite choice for late-winter indoor arrangements.

1 To force blooms, cut heavily budded branches in winter with a pair of sharp hand pruners. Cut each branch a slightly different length than the others to give the arrangement an artistic flair.

2 Arrange the branches in a vase of room-temperature water with a few stems of forsythia, which blooms at the same time, and set in a sunny window.

3 Be sure to place the vase away from heat vents that can dry out stems. Spritz the stems each day to give them extra humidity.

4 In a few days to weeks, depending on the time of year, the buds will begin to swell. Be sure to change the water in the vase every other day to keep flowers fresh for as long as possible.

PURPLE SMOKEBUSH
Cotinus coggygria

Zones: 5–8

Type: Deciduous

Light: Full to part sun

Size: 10–15 ft. tall, 10–15 ft. wide

Uses: Shrub border, specimen

Interest: Smokelike summer flower stalks; colorful foliage

Vibrant foliage and feathery plumes of purple smoke-bush make it one of the best landscape shrubs for a color accent in a lawn or garden. Its deep reddish purple foliage, the darkest of all smokebushes, explodes into an incomparable display of brilliant autumn hues. This is among the last shrubs to leaf out in spring; the foliage emerges along its brownish purple stems in mid- to late spring. Tiny yellow flowers appear after the foliage, then drop in early summer. Dusty pink, silken flower stalks take their place, forming the feathery haze that gives smokebush its common name.

HOW TO GROW
Purple smokebush is an undemanding plant, adapting easily to all but the soggiest of soils. Once established, it endures long summer droughts, dry rocky sites, and the

toughest urban conditions. Full sun promotes the richest colors, with plants in part shade only slightly less vibrant. Avoid over-fertilizing and drastic pruning, both of which promote unattractive, whiplike stems. If space is a problem, smokebush can be grown like a perennial. Cut the plant to the ground in late winter. In spring, vigorous 3- to 5-foot shoots appear, transforming smokebush into a plant that can be easily integrated into a small garden.

LANDSCAPE USE

With its upright branching habit, purple smokebush is irregularly shaped and combines well with more symmetrical, arching or rounded shrubs. The rich color and texture of purple smokebush is a good foil for shrubs with pale green or silvery gray foliage. For a sharp contrast, site it near evergreens such as yew. Its greatest landscape value is evident when purple smokebush is combined with other shrubs in a mixed border and underplanted with low ground covers and perennials.

Top Choices

- C. 'Velvet Cloak' has rich purple foliage that maintains its vibrant color throughout the growing season. The leaves turn a bold reddish purple in the fall.

- C. 'Royal Purple' grows 10 to 15 feet tall with violet foliage the color of grape jelly. In mid- to late summer, the tips of its stems are decorated with puffs of smoky flower stalks.

SMOKY PURPLE ACCENTS

Use purple smokebush to greatest advantage by featuring it in a mixed planting rather than alone as a specimen. It mixes equally well with taller shrubs, small trees, perennials, and ground covers.

- Combine purple smokebush with plants that have gray or silver foliage, such as weeping blue spruce (*Picea pungens* 'Pendula'), lavender cotton (*Santolina chamaecyparissus*), Jerusalem sage (*Phlomis fruticosa*), and English lavender (*Lavandula angustifolia*).

- Prune the lower branches to achieve a small, multi-stemmed tree as a focal point for spreading cotoneaster (*Cotoneaster divaricatus*), a clump of blue ornamental grass such as blue oat grass (*Helictotrichon sempervirens*) or blue dune grass (*Leymus condensatus* 'Canyon Prince'), and a carpet bugle (*Ajuga reptans*) ground cover.

COTONEASTER
Cotoneaster spp.

Zones: 3–8 (varies by species)

Type: Evergreen or deciduous

Light: Full to part sun

Size: Varies by species

Uses: Foundation planting, ground cover, shrub border

Interest: Spring flowers; colorful fall foliage and berries

The various cotoneasters are among the most valuable hardy garden shrubs. These diverse plants range from low-growing ground covers to spreading, bushy shrubs. Nearly every landscape benefits from the appealing architectural patterns, showy fruits, and glossy leaves these plants bring to the garden. Whether used as bank covers, foundation plants, or towering shrubs, these vigorous plants flawlessly blend their attractive appearance with easy care, making them valuable to every gardener.

HOW TO GROW
Cotoneasters are among the most tolerant of garden shrubs. Given good drainage, they flourish in almost any soil and site, withstanding wind, pollution, and other insults. For best performance, do not fertilize; water moderately. To avoid pruning, which destroys cotoneaster's

natural grace, choose a cotoneaster whose size and habit are suited to your garden. Shrubs do need occasional shaping when wayward branches appear. Remove old and weak branches to maintain vigorous growth.

Top Choices

- *C. divaricatus,* spreading cotoneaster, reaches 5 to 6 feet tall and is very easy to grow. It has the most richly colored green foliage of all cotoneasters. After bloom, its slender branches are covered with bright red berries that last into winter. Zones 5 to 8.

- *C. horizontalis,* rock cotoneaster, is widely grown and easily recognized by the herringbone pattern of its branches. It never needs pruning and its low, spreading habit is most beautifully displayed clambering over rocks or spilling over walls. Zones 4 to 7.

- *C. lacteus,* red clusterberry, grows to 9 feet tall with evergreen leaves and with long-lasting clusters of scarlet fruit. It has an imposing natural form that is attractive espaliered or pruned to expose the twisted lower branches. Zones 6 to 8.

- *C. multiflorus,* many-flowered cotoneaster, is prized for its mantle of snow white spring blossoms. It develops an arching, nearly weeping form to 10 feet tall with abundant red fruits in fall. Zones 3 to 7.

- *C. salicifolius,* willowleaf cotoneaster, is one of the tallest, reaching 10 feet. Mix this with other shrubs to thicken deep, screening borders. Zones 6 to 8.

LOW AND SPREADING

Popular *C. dammeri,* bearberry cotoneaster, is one of the very best shrubby ground covers. Its trailing branches root as they grow, making it valuable for mass plantings, on slopes, and in locations where fast growth is desired. Zones 5 to 8.

More matlike in habit, *C. adpressus,* creeping cotoneaster, is a ground-hugging, evergreen favorite. Its small, dark green foliage and rich red fruits make it an excellent low cover, especially in rock gardens. Zones 4 to 7.

C. microphyllus, little-leaf cotoneaster, is strikingly diminutive in the scale of its flowers, fruits, leaves, and stems. The variety 'Emerald Spray' produces fountains of spreading evergreen leaves with a low, arching habit. Zones 5 to 8.

WARMINSTER BROOM

Cytisus x praecox

Zones: 5–9

Type: Deciduous, with evergreen stems

Light: Full sun

Size: 3–5 ft. tall, 4–6 ft. wide

Uses: Shrub border, screen, rock garden

Interest: Spring flowers; slender gray-green leaves and stems

One of the most eye-catching sights in the spring garden is Warminster broom in full flower. Its pendulous green branches are smothered with creamy yellow blossoms, transforming this dense green shrub into a buttery fountain. Long-lasting blossoms resemble sweet peas and exude a faint odor that people either love or hate. Slender green leaves drop from the stems after a brief appearance in spring, leaving behind a bushy mound of gray-green branches. The leafless stems provide a valuable textural contrast to garden schemes and a unique dimension and color to winter landscapes.

HOW TO GROW

Adaptable and carefree, Warminster broom tolerates both coastal and inland conditions, including wind, smog, heat, and some drought. It thrives in poor, infertile, sandy soil without supplemental fertilizers as well as in heavy clay if you give it improved drainage. Alkaline soil causes broom's deep green stems to yellow.

When planting in groups, set broom plants 4 feet apart. Once planted, broom does best if left undisturbed. Prune each year after flowering to keep plants compact and prevent seedpod formation, which detracts from the attractiveness of the slender green branches. Broom is often short-lived, especially in southern climates, and may need replacing after a few years. However, the plants are so exquisite in bloom, that replanting is worth the effort.

LANDSCAPE USE

Warminster broom is easy to use in a variety of garden situations. Bereft of foliage, the gray-green branches supply a unique textural contrast to broad-leafed and coniferous plants. In borders, its pale yellow blossoms are beautiful surrounded with deeper yellow, spring-blooming perennials and taller broad-leaved shrubs.

Top Choices

- C. 'Albus' produces abundant white blooms.

- C. 'Allgold' blooms long and heavily with flowers a rich, deep yellow.

- C. 'Gold Spear' (also known as 'Canary Bird') bears bright yellow blossoms.

- C. 'Hollandia' blooms in multiple tones of pinkish red and cream.

BLENDING BROOM INTO THE GARDEN

Complement Warminster broom's soft texture with the delicate blossoms of bush cinquefoil (*Potentilla fruticosa*) in summer, red-berried cotoneasters (*Cotoneaster* spp.) in fall, and the golden glow of American arborvitae (*Thuja occidentalis* 'Rheingold') in winter. Broom is also a useful specimen plant in a rock garden with dwarf conifers and Japanese maples, or massed for a roadside screen or a graceful bank cover.

CHOOSING PLANTS FOR THE GARDEN

Warminster broom and its varieties are hybrids and are prized in all types of gardens. Many other types of broom are not as well behaved or attractive. When selecting a broom for your landscape, be sure to purchase named varieties. Avoid Scotch broom and Portuguese broom, as these species are invasive, nuisance plants.

DAPHNE
Daphne x burkwoodii

Zones: 4–8

Type: Deciduous to evergreen

Light: Full sun to part shade

Size: 3–4 ft. tall, 3–4 ft. wide

Uses: Foundation planting, specimen

Interest: Fragrant spring blossoms; colorful fall berries

The intense, sweet fragrance of daphne's spring flowers lures gardeners to include this free-blooming shrub in their landscapes. The richly perfumed, starry flowers of the popular Burkwood's daphne appear in clusters at the tips of the branches, nearly covering the dark green leaves. Occasionally, there is a second flush of bloom in late summer. In mild climates, daphne blooms throughout winter. Although it has a reputation as a temperamental shrub, daphne is as reliable as it is beautiful—if you meet its basic growing requirements.

HOW TO GROW

All daphnes are sensitive to overwatering. They must have deep, fast-draining soil and limited summer water. For best performance, plant in raised beds in slightly acidic to neutral, loose, sandy loam. Add lime to very acidic soil until tests show a pH of 6.0 to 7.0. Add plenty of compost or leaf mold for a humus-rich planting area.

Daphnes do best in full morning sun and late-afternoon shade, especially where summers are hot. Provide a mulch over the root zone to keep the soil cool, and allow lots of space from neighboring plants to reduce competition. Daphnes form a neat, rounded shrub without pruning.

LANDSCAPE USE

If you plant these splendid shrubs in a place where they will be the center of attention, they will reward you with bountiful, fragrant flowers. Feature them in a bed near an entry or along a walkway where you can catch wafts of their heady fragrance during the bloom period. To regulate the moisture daphnes receive, keep the plants away from regularly irrigated areas such as lawns.

Top Choices

- *D.* 'Carol Mackie' grows to 3 feet with dense green foliage marked with creamy gold leaf margins. Pale pink flowers open from rose-colored buds in spring.

- *D.* 'Somerset' grows 4 feet tall and equally wide. Its branches are densely covered with deep, semi-evergreen foliage. The very fragrant late-spring flowers are cream tinged with pink.

Taylor's Tips

DAPHNES AS FOUNDATION PLANTS

Burkwood daphne can be used successfully as a foundation plant if it does not receive reflected heat or excessive moisture from roof runoff. If you plant it under a wide eave, where the soil can become too dry, water it periodically.

CAUTION: All parts of daphnes are extremely poisonous, especially the bark and berries, which can cause death if ingested. Milder reactions range from inflammation of mucous membranes to abdominal pain and convulsions. Take care to keep this magnificent plant away from areas where children play.

A SUBSTITUTE FOR COLDER REGIONS

In cold northern regions where daphnes are not hardy, a similar visual effect can be attained by planting candytuft (*Iberis sempervirens*), a tough little perennial. It produces green mounds of foliage and abundant clusters of white flowers in summer.

FIVELEAF ARALIA

Eleutherococcus sieboldianus

Zones: 4–8

Type: Deciduous

Light: Full sun to full shade

Size: 8 ft. tall, 8 ft. wide

Uses: Barrier hedge, shrub border, specimen

Interest: Green-and-white variegated leaves

Fiveleaf aralia, previously known as *Acanthopanax,* is one of the best shrubs for an urban setting. Pest- and disease-free, this tough, versatile shrub adapts well to unfavorable soil conditions, pollution, and repeated pruning. It thrives where other plants suffer. In spring to early summer, airy sprays of small, greenish white flowers are held on short stalks above leaf clusters. The variegated foliage maintains its color without scorching in sun or fading in shade. Short, curved prickles along the stems make aralia useful as a barrier hedge for keeping pets and other animals out of garden areas.

HOW TO GROW

Fiveleaf aralia will grow in nearly every type of garden situation except poorly drained locations. The plant spreads quickly; it should be planted in unamended soil in a site with lots of room to expand. Spreading can be controlled by removing unwanted suckers as they appear. For a more upright form, prune out older, arching stems to encourage new, upright ones.

LANDSCAPE USE

This shrub, prized for its variegated foliage, dresses up dry, shaded spots. It thrives beneath heavily canopied trees and among other shade-loving shrubs. It also works well in darkened nooks and shaded borders, introducing sharp contrasts with shimmering two-toned pale yellow and emerald green leaves.

For a free-form barrier hedge along a garden perimeter or property line, set plants 5 feet apart and allow suckers to fill in spaces between plants. Prune as necessary to maintain desired height and width. Left unpruned, fiveleaf aralia will develop wide, draping contours. Repeated trimming keeps plants low and compact.

Top Choices

- *E. henryi,* Henry's aralia, grows to 8 feet with abundant, strong stems, rough green leaves, and late-spring to early-summer flowers that yield large, black fruits. Zones 5 to 7.

- *E. henryi* 'Nana' produces thick tangles of 4-foot-tall stems, excellent for barrier hedges. Zones 5 to 7.

FILLING A HEDGE WITH DIVISIONS

Fill in a row of widely spaced aralias by planting the empty space with divisions from already established plants.

1 Watch for suckers near the base of the plant or coming from roots some distance away.

2 Dig up the divisions while the plants are dormant in fall or very early spring. Wear sturdy gloves to protect yourself from the downward prickles on the stems.

3 Use a sharp spade to make a sharp cut through the roots that connect sucker to mother plant. Use a trowel or spade to lift as many roots as possible with soil.

4 Set transplants into the hedgerow. If the top growth has budded out and is limp, cut stems back by one-third.

ENKIANTHUS
Enkianthus campanulatus

Zones: 5–7

Type: Deciduous

Light: Part shade

Size: 10–15 ft. tall (shorter in cold climates), 8 ft. wide

Uses: Shrub border, specimen

Interest: Spring flowers; colorful fall foliage

Grown mostly for the brilliance of its fall foliage, enkianthus is also a spring beauty. Maturing into a broad, vaselike shape, the plant develops a lovely silhouette of tiered branches extending nearly horizontally from the stems. The leaves turn a vivid orange-red in fall, providing unforgettable autumn color. In late spring, pretty bell- or urn-shaped blossoms, reminiscent of lily-of-the-valley, dangle in clusters beneath tufts of leaves. Red veins accent the creamy yellow flowers.

HOW TO GROW
Enkianthus is easy to grow if planted in well-drained, acidic, humus-rich loam. It prefers the same conditions as other acid-loving shrubs such as rhododendrons. Add ground bark and an acidifying fertilizer to improve the nutrient base in poor sand or clay soils. It is best to plant

enkianthus in a permanent location when it is young; do not move it since it does not transplant readily after it is established.

Site enkinanthus in partial shade. Keep the root zone evenly moist but not wet, and add a layer of pine-bark or pine-needle mulch each spring. Prune and remove dead or broken branches as needed.

LANDSCAPE USE

Give enkianthus a place of honor in your landscape, placing it where its graceful shape and dynamic fall foliage have prominence. This is an ideal shrub to feature as a specimen in a shady lawn or set at the edge of a woodland. Its narrow base and broad top make it an excellent choice for a tiered border. The open branching provides dappled shade for underplanting perennials and low shrubs. Choose acid-loving companions such as rhododendrons, azaleas, mountain laurels and skimmias, leucothoes, and pieris. Buy plants in fall after the leaves have turned since there seems to be a great deal of variation in foliage color.

Top Choices

- *E.* 'Hollandia' has large, creamy yellow flowers with red veins.

- *E.* 'Red Bells' bears flowers that are deeper red than the species.

- *E.* 'Sikokianus' produces dark burgundy buds that reveal solid red, bell-shaped flowers etched with pink.

- *E.* 'Weston Pink' has rosy pink flowers.

POSITIONING THE ROOTBALL

When planting enkianthus, proper placement of the rootball is important to avoid disease problems and encourage vigorous growth.

1 Keep the rootball from settling after you backfill the hole by excavating an area slightly shallower than the depth of the rootball and slightly deeper around the perimeter. This provides a solid base on which to set the plant.

2 Position the rootball carefully in the planting hole, setting the top flush with surrounding soil.

3 After filling the hole with soil, water well and cover the root zone with a 2-inch-thick layer of bark chips or pine needles.

BURNING BUSH
Euonymus alata

Zones: 3–8

Type: Deciduous

Light: Full sun to full shade

Size: 8–10 ft. tall, 10 ft. wide

Uses: Foundation or mass planting, hedge, shrub border, specimen

Interest: Colorful fall foliage and berries

Blazing fall color and a versatile, low-maintenance character make burning bush one of the best all-around shrubs. The deep green summer foliage turns crimson in fall, creating a glorious autumn display. The bright orange fruit persists through winter, attracting birds and lending color to the winter garden. Hardy, resilient, and vigorous, burning bush (also known as winged euonymus) first produces upright, twiggy branches trimmed with cork-textured winged edges. In maturity, the plants become broad, vase-shaped shrubs with attractive spreading branches.

HOW TO GROW

Burning bush needs average conditions to grow well. It prospers in sun or any degree of shade but the brightest fall color comes from plants in full sun. Be sure that the soil is well drained and regular water is available. Dense, shallow roots make it difficult for other plants to grow underneath burning bush, so keep the soil bare at least to the drip line and cover it with a 2-inch layer of organic mulch such as compost or chipped bark. No pruning is required.

LANDSCAPE USE

Burning bush is an excellent specimen for a lawn or at the edge of a wooded area. It can also be grown as a clipped or unclipped barrier hedge. When left unpruned, it grows wide, especially handsome, spreading tiers of horizontal branches.

The bright red tones of burning bush are difficult to blend with other highly colored fall trees and shrubs. Try planting it with birch, ginkgo, and dawn redwood, which produce yellow fall foliage, and with evergreens. Dwarf varieties are excellent for mass plantings and combine well with Siberian carpet cypress or creeping junipers.

Top Choices

- *E.* 'Angelica' has dense branching and a tidy, compact habit.

- *E.* 'Compacta' grows 6 feet tall with smaller wings and brilliant red fall foliage. Zones 4 to 8.

- *E.* 'October Glory' has a round, compact habit with vivid scarlet fall foliage.

- *E.* 'Rudy Haag' is one of the most compact burning bush varieties, reaching 4 feet tall. It has rose-pink fall foliage.

AVOIDING EUONYMUS TROUBLES

Few plants match burning bush for ease of care and versatility. This shrub looks great for years and pests and diseases don't bother it. Burning bush is not the only *Euonymus* sold in nurseries and garden centers, just the only one that isn't troubled by pests and diseases. Some of the others, along with their strengths and weaknesses, include:

- European euonymus (*Euonymus europaea*). This is a deciduous species with good fall color and attractively colored fruits. The plants are prone to scale (small sucking insects that weaken and kill plants).

- Winter creeper (*Euonymus fortunei*). A creeping, evergreen shrub with hundreds of varieties offering colorful leaves, this is a popular plant even though it is subject to scale infestations and a disease called crown gall.

- Japanese euonymus (*Euonymus japonica*). This shrub has evergreen leaves on upright, 10-foot-tall stems. The plants are also prone to scale infestations as well as many other diseases.

FORSYTHIA
Forsythia x *intermedia*

Zones: 4–8

Type: Deciduous

Light: Full sun

Size: 7–10 ft. tall,
12–15 ft. wide

Uses: Hedge, shrub
border, specimen

Interest: Spring flowers; colorful fall foliage

For many gardeners, the cheery, canary yellow blossoms of forsythia are the very essence of spring. In warm climates, blossoms often appear in late winter. Individual forsythias can vary in form, but most have upright stems that bend to the ground. Out of bloom, forsythia blends into the background with other summer greenery and waits until spring to be noticed again. Regardless of the season, forsythia is easy to grow in a wide range of conditions.

HOW TO GROW
Forsythia is grown primarily for its bright yellow blooms, so locate it in a sunny site for the best flowering. The plant will grow in shade, but the blossoms will be pale and few in number. Average moisture and almost any soil suit this undemanding shrub. Planting bareroot

should be done in winter or very early spring, but container-grown specimens can be planted any time the soil is workable. To preserve the charm of forsythia's arching form as well as stimulate production of new wood and improve flowering, remove one-third of the oldest canes from the plant base each year after blossoming.

LANDSCAPE USE

Plant forsythia among other deciduous shrubs and near open-branched trees where it can provide welcome color in spring. Be sure to give it plenty of room to spread. Flower buds of some forsythias are not hardy north of Zone 6. In northern areas, choose hardy varieties to ensure flowering after tough winters.

Top Choices

- *F.* 'Goldzauber' bears huge numbers of lightly fragrant, golden blossoms in spring.

- *F.* 'Lynwood Gold' is a reliable variety with abundant butter-gold flowers that open in early spring.

- *F.* 'Meadowlark', 'New Hampshire Gold', 'Northern Gold', and 'Northern Sun' are recently introduced varieties that bloom well even after cold winters. All flower reliably as far north as Zone 4.

- *F.* 'Spectabilis' has been the most popular variety for decades. It has bright yellow blossoms and strong, pliant stems.

- *F.* 'Spring Glory' bears chromium yellow flowers on 6-foot-tall stems.

NEW PLANTS FROM LAYERING

Long, slender forsythia branches naturally arch over, with their tips often reaching the ground. As stems continue to grow, they frequently develop roots at leaf nodes that touch the soil.

You can promote tip layering by pegging branch ends just beneath the ground in early summer and keeping the rooting area moist.

By fall, the layered stems will be ready to transplant. Cut them once when they are well rooted, then dig them up and replant them. The new shrubs will be identical to the original plant.

LARGE FOTHERGILLA

Fothergilla major

Zones: 5–8 and milder parts of Zone 4

Type: Deciduous

Light: Full to part sun

Size: 6–10 ft. tall, 8–10 ft. wide

Uses: Shrub border, specimen

Interest: Fragrant spring blossoms; colorful fall foliage

Large fothergilla's fragrant flowers, vivid fall color, and easy-care nature make it a splendid plant for residential landscapes. Admired for splashy yellow, orange, red, and purple fall hues, its honey-scented, bottle-brush-shaped spring flowers are especially appealing. A slow-growing shrub, large fothergilla attains a height of 10 feet after many years. Given proper growing conditions, the plants are trouble-free, providing excellent fall color even in warm climates.

HOW TO GROW

For protection from hot summer sun in warm regions, plant large fothergilla in a lightly shaded site. Choose a sunny spot for best fall color in northern areas. Soil should be loose, acidic, and well drained. Amend with peat moss before planting to establish acidity and hold moisture. Mulch with pine bark or pine needles in spring. Avoid planting in dry or heavy soil. Pruning and other maintenance regimes are generally unnecessary, though vigor and flowering improve if the oldest branches are removed every few years immediately after flowering.

LANDSCAPE USE

With fuzzy spring blossoms that look like short bottle brushes, dark green leaves in summer, and dazzling fall foliage, fothergilla is a choice shrub for adding three-season interest to shrub or perennial borders. In slightly shaded sites, plant large fothergilla with azaleas and rhododendrons or use it as a substitute for these traditional plants. In sunnier spots, plant it with deciduous magnolias or Japanese maples and treelike shrubs such as winter hazel. Its fall foliage, with multicolored, mosaic patterns on nearly every leaf, is its best attribute, and makes a stunning contrast coupled with evergreen trees and shrubs. It seems even more spectacular when you plant several of these shrubs together.

Top Choice

- *F.* 'Huntsman' is a variety introduced from Europe with showy spikes of white flowers and green leaves that turn vivid shades of red in fall.

FOTHERGILLA FOR SMALL SPACES

Dwarf fothergilla, *F. gardenii*, grows about 3 to 4 feet tall and wide. Like *F. major*, this species also bears bristly, fragrant flower clusters in midspring and has magnificent fall foliage. Individual plants may slowly spread by suckering while others remain a compact mound.

Dwarf fothergilla makes an excellent low foundation plant or an accent in a large rock garden. Some of the best dwarf fothergillas include the following varieties:

- 'Blue Mist' has foliage that is blue-green and turns to vibrant shades of red, orange, and yellow in fall. In spring, the tips of its tall branches are decorated with fragrant white flowers.

- 'Jane Platt' grows only 3 feet tall and has narrow green leaves that turn orange-yellow in fall.

- 'Mount Airy' has a more upright habit, reaching 5 feet tall with abundant flower spikes and foliage that changes to bright shades of orange, red, and yellow in fall.

WITCH HAZEL
Hamamelis x *intermedia*

Zones: 5–8

Type: Deciduous

Light: Part sun

Size: Slow-growing to 15–20 ft. tall, 10–15 ft. wide

Uses: Shrub border, specimen, woodland planting

Interest: Fragrant blossoms in late winter or early spring; colorful fall foliage

The blossoms of witch hazel are one of the earliest signs of spring in the garden. The flowers have many long, narrow petals and cling to leafless gray branches like dozens of yellow, gold, or rusty red spiders. The all-around best choice is the hybrid *H.* x *intermedia*. Seemingly oblivious to frosts and snow, the fragrant blossoms of witch hazel can linger for many weeks from late winter to spring. The overall effect looks like a wonderfully delicate oriental flower arrangement. In fall, the attractive green leaves turn vibrant shades of yellow, gold, and red.

HOW TO GROW

Witch hazel is not a fussy shrub and adapts to a wide variety of conditions. It does best in well-drained, acidic soil with abundant leaf mold or organic matter. Witch hazel prefers a moist location with morning or late-afternoon sun. Mulch around the root zone to help keep the soil cool in the South and inhibit frost heaving in the North. Witch hazel develops a pleasing shape without pruning, but do cut a few budded branches for fragrant indoor bouquets.

LANDSCAPE USE

At home in dappled woodland shade, this hardy shrub is also reliable in urban settings since it tolerates pollution. Witch hazel's upright branching is perfect for underplanting with clumps of Siberian squill, narcissus, hellebore, and cyclamen, or, in mild climates, with heaths and heathers. For summer interest, try adding annual sweet peas or a large-flowered clematis to climb up and cascade down into the branches. Witch hazel's autumn color partners beautifully with fiery maples, sour gums, and dogwoods.

Top Choices

- *H.* 'Arnold's Promise' is a late-blooming, long-flowering cultivar with large, bright yellow flowers, lovely green foliage, and mottled fall color; it grows to 20 feet.

- *H.* 'Diane' has copper-colored flowers and scarlet-maroon fall foliage on plants that are more compact than other varieties.

- *H.* 'Primavera' and 'Sunburst' bear heavy crops of superb yellow blossoms and grow 10 to 15 feet tall.

- *H.* 'Winter Beauty' has dark orange, very fragrant flowers.

MORE WITCH HAZELS

There are many different types of witch hazel, including species native to America and more exotic types introduced from Asia. They are all easy to grow and provide attractive flowers and colorful fall foliage. A few more choices to consider:

- *H. virginiana,* a loose, open-growing American native, is hardy from Zones 4 to 8. It has yellow fall foliage that often drops just as the yellow flowers make their appearance.

- *H. vernalis,* spring witch hazel, grows to 10 feet with dark green leaves that turn sunny yellow in fall. The red to yellow blossoms appear in late winter in the South and in early spring in the North. Zones 4 to 8.

- *H. mollis,* Chinese witch hazel, bears yellow-and-red, very fragrant blossoms in early spring. Its medium green leaves turn soft yellow in fall. Zones 5 to 8.

ROSE-OF-SHARON
Hibiscus syriacus

Zones: 5–9

Type: Deciduous

Light: Full sun

Size: 8–15 ft. tall, 5 ft. wide

Uses: Container plant, hedge, shrub border, specimen

Interest: Midsummer flowers

This charming, old-fashioned shrub bears large, splashy blossoms that are highlights of the garden in late summer. The showy flowers resemble large single, semidouble, or double hollyhocks, depending on the variety. The pastel solid colors are sometimes marked with an eye—a contrasting splotch of color at the center of each blossom—that makes the flowers stand out against the shiny, dark green leaves. Rose-of-Sharon can be trained to a single stem as a tree but it is more commonly grown as a multi-stemmed shrub with upright, somewhat stiff tan-gray branches.

HOW TO GROW
Rose-of-Sharon is an adaptable shrub that tolerates poor soil and some dryness, but it prefers moist, well-drained, humus-rich soil. It grows well in coastal conditions.

With a little extra care, you can manipulate this shrub for dense growth and heavy flowering. Fertilize twice a year with a balanced, all-purpose fertilizer—once in early spring and again in midsummer. Cut back shoots by one-third in late winter or early spring to encourage bushiness and more flowering stems. Rose-of-Sharon leafs out in late spring. Any winter-killed wood is often not recognizable until then. Spider mites are sometimes a problem in warm, humid weather.

LANDSCAPE USE

A beautiful addition to a mixed border, rose-of-Sharon is also ideal for making a colorful privacy hedge or screen. Allow a spring-blooming clematis vine to intertwine through a freestanding shrub for spring and early-summer color until the shrub begins its midsummer flower show. Rose-of-Sharon is also a nice specimen plant to use as an accent in old-fashioned gardens.

Top Choices

- *H.* 'Aphrodite' bears medium pink flowers splashed with red in the center.

- *H.* 'Diana' has beautiful, pure white blooms and dark green leaves.

- *H.* 'Helene' boasts flowers of satin white, each splashed with a reddish purple eye.

- *H.* 'Minerva' has slightly ruffled petals. Blooms are lavender-pink with a reddish purple eye.

A TROPICAL DELIGHT

An outdoor plant only in Zone 10, tropical hibiscus (*H. rosa-sinensis*) boasts larger, showier flowers than rose-of-Sharon. Blossoms can reach 4 to 6 inches across and appear continuously all year long, although individual flowers last for only a day.

At planting time, provide a sunny spot and excellent drainage, whether planting tropical hibiscus in the ground or in pots. To ensure healthy growth and blossoming, lightly fertilize each month; twice a month if plants are in containers. Prune young plants to give good structure, then cut out one-third of the old wood each spring. Pinch stem tips in spring for best flowering. This tender shrub needs careful protection from frosts.

ROSE-OF-SHARON ON THE PATIO

Choose a narrow-growing variety or a tree form for planting in the corner of a patio or courtyard. The upright branches are perfectly suited for underplanting or growing in pots.

OAKLEAF HYDRANGEA
Hydrangea quercifolia

Zones: 5–9

Type: Deciduous

Light: Full sun to part shade

Size: 4–8 ft. tall, 6–8 ft. wide

Uses: Mass planting, shrub border, specimen

Interest: Summer flowers; colorful fall foliage

Oakleaf hydrangea is a broad, handsome shrub with dramatic, highly textured foliage like oak leaves. Young shrubs are narrow and upright but take on a graceful, rounded form as they mature. This shrub remains good-looking through all four seasons. Pairs of pale green, folded spring leaves deepen to dark green as they open. In summer, the panicles of pure white flowers gently age to dusty pink. Ruddy orange and burgundy tones envelop the foliage in fall, and the attractive, cinnamon-colored bark is visible all winter long.

HOW TO GROW
All hydrangeas like rich, well-drained, evenly moist, slightly acidic soil. They grow best in filtered light or afternoon shade but also grow well in full sun. To shape

this shrub, prune back stems by one-third to one-half as flowers fade, removing the oldest stems at the base. Buds will form at branch tips for next year's flowers. Maintain plants growing in small spaces by limiting the number of stems. In the coldest zones, protect young plants from winter damage. Temperatures below -10°F, however, can prevent flowering on an oakleaf hydrangea of any age, in which case it becomes a foliage shrub for the current year.

LANDSCAPE USE

Oakleaf hydrangea is an exceptional plant to feature in a foliage garden for its bold leaf shape and texture. From a distance, the white flower panicles light up a shade garden in late summer. Use in a mass planting as an anchor at the end of a shrub border, or place at the foot of a grassy slope or at the edge of a woodland in company with dogwood and mountain laurel.

Top Choices

- *H. quercifolia* 'Snowflake' has unique floral clusters whose petals appear double. The flowers are especially large and icy white.

- *H. macrophylla* 'Pia' is a dwarf bigleaf hydrangea that stands only 2 feet tall. Its flowers are a rich pink, even in acidic soil.

- *H. paniculata* 'Tardiva' bears elegant clusters of white blossoms from late summer to early fall.

MOPHEAD OR LACECAP

More commonly grown than the oakleaf species, bigleaf hydrangea's (*H. macrophylla*) bright flowers come in two types: mophead (above right) or lacecap (above left). Acidic soil (pH 5.0–5.5) causes blue or purple blossoms. Alkaline soil produces pink or red flowers. Zones 6 to 9.

OLD-FASHIONED HYDRANGEAS

Many people's favorite hydrangea is an old-fashioned variety called peegee hydrangea (*Hydrangea paniculata* 'Grandiflora'). This fast-growing, vase-shaped shrub has coarse-textured leaves and large clusters of white flowers in summer. In fall, the flowers turn pinkish while the foliage becomes bronze-purple. The dried flowers make bold additions to indoor arrangements. Zones 4 to 8.

HYPERICUM
Hypericum 'Hidcote'

Zones: 6–9 and milder parts of Zone 5

Type: Semi-evergreen

Light: Full to part sun

Size: 3–4 ft. tall, 3 ft. wide

Uses: Ground cover, hedge, mass planting, shrub border

Interest: Summer flowers; colorful fall foliage

The sunny yellow shrub hypericum, also called St.-John's-wort, is a relative of the ancient herb and common ground cover. 'Hidcote' is one of the best of the hypericums and brings bright color, ease of care, and mild fragrance to the garden all summer long. Its showy blossoms, with their saucer-shaped, waxy flowers decorated with tufts of yellow stamens, are larger than those of most hypericums. This shrub makes an excellent addition to the summer garden.

HOW TO GROW

Hypericum does well in average conditions as well as hot, dry, sandy soil. It does best, however, in a well-drained site in full to part sun. In cold climates, shoots often die back to the ground in winter. They will regrow from the crown in spring, producing flowers at the tips of new growth in summer. 'Hidcote' is usually not troubled by pests or diseases, though in some parts of the South it sometimes suffers from a wilt-like disease. To control this problem, remove and discard any infected plants.

LANDSCAPE USE

One of the best shrubs for planting in masses, 'Hidcote' hypericum can be used as a small-area ground cover or low hedge. Use the yellow-flowered hummocks to break up broad sweeps of lower, dense covers. The plants thrive near the seashore and are excellent additions to summertime coastal gardens. In shrub borders, they fit nicely into corners created by larger plants and also work well as a frame for taller shrubs. Plant 'Hidcote' hypericum among perennials or as a filler wherever bright summer color is needed.

Top Choices

- *H. androsaemum* 'Albury Purple' grows to 3 feet with yellow summer flowers and dark green leaves that are purple when young. Zones 5 to 9.

- *H. androsaemum* 'Autumn Blaze' features stunning fall foliage in shades of red, orange, and yellow. Zones 5 to 9.

- *H.* x *inodorum* 'Elstead' has pale yellow flowers on a tidy, compact plant. Zones 6 to 10.

Taylor's Tips

ANNUAL
RENEWAL

By treating 'Hidcote' hypericum like a perennial and cutting all stems to the ground each spring, you will generate vigorous new growth of succulent, twiggy red stems. This radical pruning produces the heaviest flowering and keeps the shrub bushy and small, usually below 2 feet. If renewed annually in this manner, 'Hidcote' hypericum is quite at home in perennial borders.

HARDIER
HYPERICUMS

Shrubby St.-John's-wort, *H. prolificum*, is hardy to Zone 3. It is a small, dense shrub, 1 to 4 feet tall and wide, that adapts to hot, dry, heavy soil as well as alkalinity. *H. kalmianum*, Kalm St.-John's-wort, is hardy to Zone 4 and adapts to rocky sites. Both of these attractive shrubs have a bluish green cast to the foliage and make lovely additions to colorful borders as well as difficult sites.

CHINESE HOLLY
Ilex cornuta

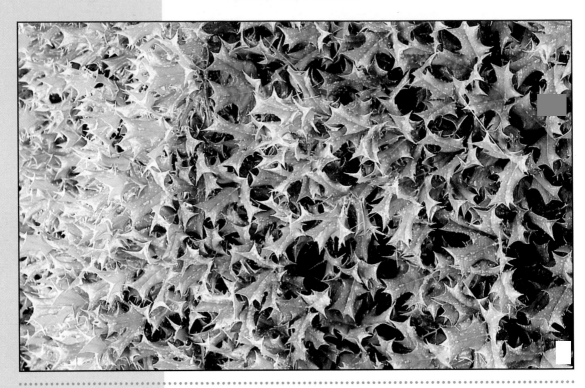

Zones: 7–9; with protection in Zone 6

Type: Evergreen

Light: Full to part sun

Size: 8–10 ft.tall, 8–10 ft. wide

Uses: Foundation planting, barrier hedge, specimen

Interest: Evergreen leaves; colorful fall berries

Chinese holly is one of the most versatile of the evergreen hollies, thriving in heat and drought where many other hollies fail. It typically flourishes in mild-winter climates through long months of warm weather that encourage a profusion of decorative red fruits. Some varieties bear lustrous, dark green foliage similar to the classic holly leaf of winter holidays, while others bear smooth-edged leaves. All are appealing and dependable plants that can serve as the backbone of a landscape year after year.

HOW TO GROW

Grow Chinese holly in full sun for plentiful berries and compact growth. This durable shrub can take heavy soil and tough conditions, though it prefers slightly acidic loam and even moisture. At planting time, take note of winter exposure, sheltering it from drying winter winds and damaging winter sun. Irrigate in fall if the soil is dry to provide soil moisture before the ground freezes.

Generally disease-resistant, Chinese holly can be damaged by certain fungal diseases. Keep irrigation water away from the trunk to prevent excessive moisture from collecting near the crown. If scale is a problem, spray with a lightweight horticultural oil.

LANDSCAPE USE

A workhorse shrub, Chinese holly is one of the most impenetrable and attractive barrier plants. Unpruned, it forms a dense thicket. You can control the size of most cultivars through clipping. Some varieties such as 'Carissa' are so slow-growing that they never require pruning. All make a useful evergreen background for perennials. Several varieties of Chinese holly can be combined for a variety of uses, from low foundation plantings to taller corner posts.

Top Choices

- *I.* 'Burfordii' grows to 20 feet with nearly spineless leaves and lavish red fruit clusters that develop without a male plant.

- *I.* 'Dwarf Burford' has a compact habit, reaching 10 feet tall, with glossy leaves and bright red berries that develop without a male plant.

- *I.* 'Carissa' is a compact plant with glossy rounded leaves. It does not bear fruit.

- *I.* 'Grandview' is a compact, male (non-fruiting) variety with small, glossy green leaves.

GETTING A BUSH FULL OF BERRIES

Most holly plants bear either male or female flowers and require a pollinator for the best berry production. Many varieties of Chinese holly set berries without a pollinator (male plant).

If you grow other types of hollies and want to guarantee berries, you must plant a female shrub as only they produce berries. It is best to plant a male and female of the same species to ensure flowering at the same time, necessary for pollination.

Most self-pollinating varieties produce even more berries with a male plant nearby.

HOLLIES FOR NORTHERN GARDENS

Meserve hybrid hollies (*Ilex x meserveae*) combine cold hardiness and attractive evergreen leaves. The plants have spiny, dark green foliage and showy red berries. 'Blue Princess' has dense foliage and abundant clusters of berries. Plant 'Blue Stallion', a male variety, nearby for proper pollination and best berry production. Zones 5 to 9.

WINTERBERRY
Ilex verticillata

Zones: 3–9

Type: Deciduous

Light: Full to part sun

Size: 10 ft. tall, 10 ft. wide

Uses: Mass planting, shrub border, wildlife garden

Interest: Colorful fall and winter berries

One of the few deciduous hollies, winterberry, with its scarlet-red berries, is also one of the best-loved shrubs for enlivening the winter landscape. The bare stems of this hardiest of hollies are the perfect stage for the glorious display of vermilion berries, especially when viewed against a backdrop of snow. Lacking the leaf spines characteristic of the classic evergreen holly, winterberry has thin, lightly serrated, elliptical leaves. This shrub can be trained into a multi-stemmed small tree or left unpruned to develop a broad, rounded crown. It grows more slowly in the North.

HOW TO GROW
Native to swampy habitats high in organic matter and acidity, winterberry is one of the few hollies to thrive in wet conditions. Grow it in sun or part shade. These

slow-growing plants do best in moist, fertile soil. To enrich poor soil, work in compost, peat moss, or leaf mold. Make an annual application of an all-purpose, balanced fertilizer in spring. Prune shrubby forms to force new growth. Remove lower branches from upright forms for the same reason.

LANDSCAPE USE

This profusely fruited species is spectacular when planted in masses against a light or dark background. Select a planting site for winterberry where you can enjoy it from indoors during the winter. Bird-watchers will delight in the flocks attracted to its fruits.

Add an individual winterberry to a mixed border or place one among evergreens for late-season interest. Place groups of three or more in an open area or along a creekside or pond, even where seasonal flooding occurs. Male winterberries, necessary for berry production, can be set in the background or blended into a shrub border.

Top Choices

- *I.* 'Earlibright' has bright orange-red fruit on 5-foot plants.

- *I.* 'Maryland Beauty' bears large red berries on strong stems. Both 'Earlibright' and 'Maryland Beauty' are pollinated best by male 'Jim Dandy' and also grow to a height of 5 feet.

- *I.* 'Sparkleberry' is a female hybrid variety with a rounded habit and abundant crops of crimson berries in fall. The best male pollinating variety is 'Apollo', which has the same parentage as 'Sparkleberry'.

Taylor's Tips

COLOR SCHEMES

Winterberry hollies are bedecked with a range of berry colors that may appeal to different garden color schemes. 'Aurantiaca' and 'Chrysocarpa' are admired for orange and yellow fruit, respectively, that is unattractive to birds and therefore lasts a long time on the shrubs. 'Winter Gold' bears orange berries with a pinkish tinge. 'Shaver' yields some of the largest fruit—in a beautiful shade of red-orange.

MAKE ROOM FOR TWO

If you are considering planting a winterberry, be sure to make room for two, since this is one of the hollies that requires a male pollinator. Only the female of this species yields berries. In mass plantings, one male is adequate for pollinating ten female plants.

VIRGINIA SWEETSPIRE
Itea virginica

Zones: 5–9

Type: Deciduous

Light: Full sun to part shade

Size: 3–5 ft. tall, 2–4 ft. wide

Uses: Mass planting, wildlife gardens

Interest: Fragrant summer flowers; colorful fall foliage

Virginia sweetspire is a tough native plant loved for its abundant summer flowering, showy fall colors, and usefulness in moist sites. Its upright stems have a tendency to branch mostly at their tops, fostering a draping, graceful appearance, especially in older shrubs. The pleasantly fragrant spikes of white blossoms are this species' hallmark. Varieties of Virginia sweetspire have upright or drooping stems. Bright green foliage turns vivid scarlet and purple in fall, persisting for months in all but the coldest climates.

HOW TO GROW
Trouble-free Virginia sweetspire will grow in nearly every garden. Though it prefers moist, fertile conditions, it is surprisingly drought-tolerant and adaptive. For the densest, most attractive growth, plant it in rich soil.

Locate it in full sun to part shade. As with many plants, long hours in sunlight produce more abundant flowering, fuller, more compact growth, and richer fall color. Plants in full sun should be grown in moist soil and mulched with a 2-inch layer of bark chips.

Sweetspire spreads by underground stems and sometimes needs to be controlled. (see "Root-Pruning" at right). Prune the aboveground parts sparingly.

LANDSCAPE USE

For a succession of blooms, plant sweetspire in moist, slightly shaded sites with swaths of woodland perennials such as spring-blooming columbines, Virginia bluebells, and hybrid anemones. Sweetspire's richly colored foliage adds interest throughout fall and much of winter. Given its tendency to spread, sweetspire is best used in masses for naturalizing along streams or ponds, by roadsides, or in habitually moist low spots. It looks stunning when grown in a mixed planting with summersweet.

Top Choice

• *I.* 'Henry's Garnet' is an award-winning 3- to 4-foot-high cultivar with rich red-purple fall color that lasts many weeks. Long, fragrant flower clusters decorate this attractive shrub in midsummer.

ROOT-PRUNING

Determine first how far in circumference you want a colony of Virginia sweetspire to spread. Beyond that point, cut through any expanding roots or underground stems with a sharp shovel.

Roots that do not have aboveground shoots will eventually weaken and die once they are cut off from the parent plant. Roots that have developed stems will continue to grow unless you pull up the shoots after cutting their roots.

Root-prune once in late spring and again in July or August. Remove top growth outside of the circle whenever it appears.

JUNIPER

Juniperus spp.

Zones: 2–9 (varies by species)

Type: Evergreen

Light: Full sun to light shade

Size: Varies by species

Uses: Foundation planting, ground cover, shrub border

Interest: Evergreen foliage

Junipers are a diverse group of plants that range from creeping ground covers to upright, columnar-shaped trees, with other forms in between. The large variety of shapes, hardiness, and shades of evergreen foliage ensures that some type of juniper will fit into your landscape or garden. This shrub is a favorite for its carefree nature and its ability to grow in difficult sites—those with poor soil, wind, drought, pollution, and extremes of heat and cold. When selecting a juniper, note its ultimate height and width; most species will reach their mature size in just a few years.

How to Grow

Junipers attain their best form and color when grown in full sun, except in deserts and other hot-summer climates where light shade is preferable. In heavy shade, they languish and become thin. All types thrive in either acidic or alkaline soil, as long as it is well drained. When planted in irrigated lawns or wet sites, junipers are subject to root rot. Many species survive without supplemental watering, even in high-desert climates.

LANDSCAPE USE

Low-growing junipers, such as varieties of creeping juniper (*J. horizontalis*), are suitable for massing as ground covers and for controlling erosion on steep slopes. Another low-growing species, shore juniper (*J. conferta*), is less hardy than creeping juniper but very tolerant of sand and salt spray, making it one of the best shrubs for coastal areas. Midsized junipers, including Chinese juniper (*J. chinensis*), have long, sweeping branches and grow up to 6 feet tall. Use for specimen, hedge, or foundation plants.

Top Choices

- *J. horizontalis* 'Bar Harbor' grows only 1 foot tall and spreads up to 8 feet wide. Zones 2 to 9.

- *J. horizontalis* 'Wiltonii' (also called 'Blue Rug' because of its silvery blue foliage) grows only 6 inches tall. Zones 2 to 9.

- *J. chinensis* 'Pfitzerana' is a group of juniper varieties that range from compact to tall forms and perform well in both the North and South. Zones 4 to 9.

- *J. conferta* 'Blue Pacific' is 1 foot tall with silvery blue foliage. Zones 6 to 9.

SPECIAL USES FOR JUNIPER

J. chinensis var. *procumbens* has gray-green, prickly foliage. It is an excellent ground cover for hillsides, in rock gardens, or near patios. Prune the 8-inch- to 2-foot-tall cultivars of this species to control their spreading habit. Zones 4 to 9.

J. sabina, Savin juniper, is one of the best low-growing species for urban sites. Many of its cultivars have dark green foliage and a vase-shaped form with hardiness suited to more northern climates. Zones 3 to 7.

Cultivars of Rocky Mountain junipers, *J. scopulorum*, are a diverse group, best for the Plains and Rocky Mountain states.

DISEASE-RESISTANCE

Several junipers are notable for their resistance to juniper blight, including: Sargent's juniper (*J. chinensis* var. *sargentii*) as well as the 'Broadmoor', 'Pepin', and 'Von Ehren' varieties of Savin juniper (*J. sabina*).

MOUNTAIN LAUREL
Kalmia latifolia

Zones: 4–9

Type: Evergreen

Light: Part sun to dappled shade

Size: 3–10 ft. tall, 7–10 ft. wide

Uses: Mass planting, screen, shrub border, woodland planting

Interest: Evergreen foliage; spring flowers

Native to the eastern United States, mountain laurel is one of the most exquisitely beautiful flowers in the garden. The showy bouquets of cupped blossoms begin as clusters of bright rosy red buds at the tips of branches in late spring. The buds fade as they open, revealing flowers in clear, crisp shades of white or pink. Many blossoms are marked with deep tones in their throats or bands on their petals. This slow-growing, evergreen plant has a formal, compact look when young, then gracefully ages into a more relaxed, open form.

HOW TO GROW
Success with mountain laurel depends on selecting the right site and on the care you give it at planting time. (See "Planting Mountain Laurel," far right.) A lightly shaded site with acidic conditions, similar to this shrub's

natural habitat, is critical. Thick layers of pine-bark mulch renewed annually help conserve moisture, keep the shallow roots cool, and supply organic matter. For best performance, apply a balanced, acidifying fertilizer in late winter. If mountain laurel becomes leggy and gaunt, cut it to within 6 inches of the ground to renew the entire shrub. The plant will spend several years producing new leaves and branches before again bearing flowers. It's worth the wait.

LANDSCAPE USE

Mountain laurel is a perfect choice for naturalizing beneath tall deciduous trees and is a good partner for azaleas and rhododendrons. It even thrives beneath tall hemlocks and pines, though flowering in these conditions is much reduced. It is quite handsome planted in masses or used as an accent in shaded shrub borders. Taller varieties make excellent evergreen screens and backgrounds for other plants. Dwarf forms work well in rock gardens with dwarf conifers or along foundations, as long as the soil is acidic and they do not receive reflected heat or winter sun.

Top Choices

- *K.* 'Bullseye' has white flowers banded with a ring of deep crimson.

- *K.* 'Elf' has white to pale pink flowers on 3- to 6-foot dwarf plants.

- *K.* 'Raspberry Glow' has dark red buds and reddish pink blossoms on 6-foot stems.

- *K.* 'Tiddlywinks', with deep pink blossoms, is the smallest variety at just 2 feet tall.

Taylor's Tips

FOR BEST FORM

Keep mountain laurel compact and encourage new growth with annual pruning of old wood after flowering and removal of unproductive branches. Prune to about 6 inches from the ground.

If you don't have much room, begin with dwarf, compact plants rather than relying on pruning for controlling size. Deadhead spent blooms to encourage bushiness and promote consistent flowering.

CAUTION: All parts of mountain laurel are poisonous if eaten.

PLANTING
MOUNTAIN LAUREL

Plant mountain laurel during cool weather in fall or in spring after the soil has warmed.

- Select a site with part sun or dappled shade and adjust the soil pH to 5.0 to 5.5.

- Set the rootball in a hole three times the width of the rootball. Use a porous planting mix or garden soil, generously amended with organic matter. After planting, mulch with pine needles or bark.

- Water in with an acidic fertilizer at half the recommended rate. Keep soil evenly moist.

KERRIA

Kerria japonica

Zones: 4–9

Type: Deciduous

Light: Part sun

Size: 6 ft. tall,
6 ft. wide

Uses: Ground cover,
mass planting, shrub
border

Interest: Spring flowers; colorful fall foliage

From coast to coast, kerria has become one of the most popular of all the yellow-flowered, spring-blooming shrubs. The cultivar 'Pleniflora', with double, pomponlike flowers that bloom for several weeks, is generally preferred over the species, whose flat-petaled, single blossoms are more ephemeral. 'Pleniflora' is smothered with slender sprays of yellow floral puffs in spring and lightly thereafter throughout summer. Sometimes called Japanese rose for its rose-family heritage, this cultivar is not only showier, but also more winter hardy than the species.

HOW TO GROW

After a slow start, kerria is an easy-care shrub, tolerant of nearly any soil and garden situation. It grows best in a well-drained, slightly shaded site where the flowers will hold their color longer. Avoid fertilizing except in the poorest soil as excess fertility increases growth at the expense of flowers.

Pruning improves the overall appearance and flowering of this fast-growing shrub (see "Pruning Out Deadwood" at right). Unpruned, it can become a tangle of suckering stems and branches that take root where they contact the soil surface.

LANDSCAPE USE

Kerria is an informal plant, ideal for mass plantings or mixed shrub borders where its flowers provide vivid contrast. Even in winter, its masses of bare, shiny green or yellowish green stems add color and texture to the landscape. This shrub is a good alternative to forsythia. It is especially attractive when its whiplike branches are trained along a rail fence. Also plant kerria as a colorful screen in front of walls and storage areas, or as a large-scale rambling ground cover.

Top Choices

- *K.* 'Aureo-variegata' has yellow-edged leaves and looks wonderful in mass plantings on slopes.

- *K.* 'Picta' has abundant yellow flowers and leaves attractively edged with white. It withstands sun better than most variegated shrubs.

- *K.* 'Pleniflora' has double, butter yellow flowers on vigorous stems reaching 6 to 8 feet tall.

Taylor's Tips

PRUNING OUT DEADWOOD

Although kerria will flower without pruning, it grows into an unruly tangle when left to its own devices. The plants look much better if you prune out deadwood in the center and do not allow it to become dense and twiggy.

Keep the shrub looking neat and tidy by thinning out the oldest stems at the base every year or two immediately after flowering. This will produce vigorous new growth and encourage an open habit. In early spring, shear off twigs that have been damaged by the winter cold.

COMPATIBLE PLANTS

Plant kerria against a sunny wall, setting early white tulips and pale narcissus around its lower branches. In summer, let it serve as a framework for showy ornamental grasses such as zebra and flame grass.

Many perennials, such as sedum 'Autumn Joy' and tall orange daylilies including 'No Idea' and 'Kwanzo', complement this popular shrub.

BEAUTYBUSH
Kolkwitzia amabilis

Zones: 5–8 and milder parts of Zone 4

Type: Deciduous

Light: Full sun

Size: 6–12 ft. tall, 5–8 ft. wide

Uses: Barrier hedge, screen, shrub border, specimen

Interest: Attractive bark; flowers in late spring

Small, porcelain pink flowers in 2- to 3-inch clusters cover beautybush in late spring, giving it the appearance of a floating, pastel cloud. The tremendous show of countless pink bells on arching stems is the source of its common name. On older plants, tall stems tend to arch over, fountainlike, under the weight of the blossoms. Bristly, feathery seed heads persist for several weeks after flowering, often remaining well into winter when older stems shed flakes of silvery brown bark.

How to Grow

Pest- and disease-free, beautybush is one of those seemingly self-sufficient shrubs from old-fashioned gardens. It does best in well-drained, loamy soil in sunny sites but is not fussy about conditions, tolerating both acidic and alkaline soils. To promote new growth that keeps beautybush truly beautiful, cut out two or three of the oldest stems at the base of the plants immediately after flowers fade. Cut all stems to the ground to renew a poorly shaped bush or to use among perennials.

LANDSCAPE USE

Beautybush is a very reliable shrub that never fails to live up to its name. No matter how hard the winter, this shrub always bears froths of pink blossoms in spring. It is an excellent plant for the shrub border, where it commands attention when in bloom and then blends into the background.

As a specimen, beautybush looks best with its lower branches removed to form an attractive umbrella shape. For added effect, surround beautybush with clumps of dwarf daylilies such as 'Stella de Oro' or 'Happy Returns' that bear yellow flowers all summer long. Along boundary lines or near meadows, beautybush creates a visual screen or hedge.

Top Choices

- K. 'Pink Cloud' has abundant clusters of tubular flowers, colored deep pink on the outside and soft, blush white inside. The plants have a lovely vase shape and eventually reach a height of 8 feet.

- K. 'Rosea' is similar in size and shape to 'Pink Cloud' but with reddish flowers.

ADDED BEAUTY WITH
CLIMBING ROSES

Climbing roses can complement beautybush in two ways: by climbing through the shrub to extend the flowering season by growing next to it to provide a colorful summer background.

Climbing roses planted at the base of beautybush can ramble through the branches, its canes following the form of the shrub's stems. Select the simple beauty of a single-flowered rose, such as blush white 'Sally Holmes' or the fetching, double blossoms of pale pink 'New Dawn'.

For a different look, train the red 'William Baffin' climbing rose on a wall or trellis behind or adjacent to beautybush. Another choice is pastel pink 'Aloha', an English climber with very fragrant, double flowers.

DROOPING LEUCOTHOE
Leucothoe fontanesiana

Zones: 5–8 and milder parts of Zone 4

Type: Evergreen

Light: Part sun to full shade

Size: 3–6 ft. tall, 3–6 ft. wide

Uses: Foundation plant, mass planting, woodland planting

Interest: Evergreen foliage; spring flowers

The hardiest of its genus, drooping leucothoe bears nodding, bell-shaped spring flowers in dangling clusters along slender, arching stems. This shade-loving shrub is a relative of rhododendrons and pieris and is a useful companion to both. Its evergreen leaves and leafy stems give it a flowing, willowy appearance. The lustrous foliage, which turns purple-green in winter, is a fine addition to bouquets.

HOW TO GROW

Grow drooping leucothoe in a sheltered location with moist, acidic soil and plenty of organic matter. Given these conditions, it does well in dappled to full shade in mild climates and part sun or shade elsewhere. The plant has a natural elegance and maintains its attractive appearance even when left unpruned. Pruning the oldest branches to the ground right after flowering helps keep the plant compact and vigorous.

LANDSCAPE USE

Drooping leucothoe's arching stems and evergreen foliage are lovely accents to shady perennial borders or mixed plantings of evergreens. The distinctive texture of the leaves is stunning in mass plantings. Drooping leucothoe's low, spreading habit is well suited for use along streams and winding woodland paths and at ponds' edges. This shrub also thrives in containers and adds a pleasing accent to shaded decks or terrace gardens. Given even moisture and annual root-pruning, it is a long-lasting and attractive potted shrub.

Another Leucothoe

- *L. axillaris,* coast leucothoe, is more compact than drooping leucothoe, reaching 2 to 4 feet tall. Its graceful, arching stems are covered with glossy, evergreen leaves. White, bell-shaped flowers appear in early to midspring. Coast leucothoe needs moist, acidic soil high in organic matter. It grows best when planted on the northern side of a building or in a shady mixed border of rhododendrons, pieris, and azaleas. Its cultivar, 'Compacta', grows only 2 feet tall with a densely branched, mounding habit. New growth is tinged with red, matures to a rich, glossy green, and turns a bronzy green in winter. Zones 5 to 8.

Taylor's Tips

AVOIDING STRESS

Stress induced by excessive heat and wind, drought, or poor drainage has serious repercussions for drooping leucothoe. Stressed plants are susceptible to fungal leaf spots that are not only disfiguring but can cause leaf drop and premature death. To avoid stress, give this otherwise durable shrub excellent drainage, consistent, light moisture, a cool, shady location, and humus-rich soil.

COMPLEMENTARY COMPANIONS

Set these shade-loving plants with leucothoe in groups of three to five. All thrive in a cool, woodsy setting in humus-rich soil.

- Evergreen Lenten rose (*Helleborus orientalis*) has contrasting fans of dark green foliage and pink, white, or rose-violet blooms in early spring.

- Lilac or white-flowered, variegated hostas (*Hosta* spp.) offer summer flowers and contrasting foliage.

- Black snakeroot (*Cimicifuga racemosa*) adds late-summer drama with its deep green leaves and tall stems topped with feathery spires of white flowers.

WINTER HONEYSUCKLE

Lonicera fragrantissima

Zones: 6–8 and milder
parts of Zones 5 and 9

Type: Deciduous to
semi-evergreen

Light: Full to part sun

Size: 8 ft. tall,
8 ft. wide

Uses: Hedge, screen,
shrub border,
specimen

Interest: Fragrant
early-spring flowers;
colorful summer
berries

Fast-growing winter honeysuckle is appealing for its rich fragrance and decorative blue-green foliage. It blooms in late winter in mild climates and in early spring elsewhere. Its small, creamy white blossoms are rather ordinary but they emit a most extraordinary honeysuckle scent. After flowering, red berries festoon the branches, to be devoured by birds in summer. In fall and early winter, the small leaves deepen to green or brown, then drop from the stems late in the season.

HOW TO GROW

One of easiest shrubs to grow, winter honeysuckle can fend for itself once established. With no special needs, it is amenable to a wide range of soils and thrives in average garden conditions. It does not like wet, saturated soil or extended droughts, though it can tolerate some summer dryness.

Honeysuckle needs a little pruning to look its best; if you give it a high-profile position, treat the branches to periodic light grooming immediately after flowering to give it a more manicured, presentable appearance. Prune broken or winter-damaged twigs and give arching branches a light clipping to control shape. To limit growth and encourage new stems, remove the oldest branches every few years and dig up suckering stems. New stems will quickly replace old ones.

LANDSCAPE USE

Place winter honeysuckle in a shrub border or as a hedge where you can enjoy the wonderful fragrance of the flowers over their long bloom period. Set near patios, windows, or decks, the perfume floats on the breeze, while in enclosed courtyards or entry areas, the scent lingers longer. In locales with warmer winters, plant winter honeysuckle near a bench in a garden nook for a fragrant outdoor retreat.

Top Choices

- *L. nitida*, box honeysuckle, is an evergreen shrub with a habit similar to winter honeysuckle. The plants bear small, sweetly fragrant, white flowers in spring. The scent seems strong to some people while others claim not to smell it at all. Zones 6 to 9.

- *L. nitida* 'Baggesen's Gold', a yellow-leaved cultivar, is a bold golden accent in foliage borders. Zones 6 to 9.

LOROPETALUM
Loropetalum chinense

Zones: 7–9

Type: Evergreen

Light: Part sun to part shade

Size: 5 ft. tall, 6–8 ft. wide

Uses: Shade garden, shrub border, specimen, woodland planting

Interest: Evergreen leaves; spring flowers

A relative of witch hazel, loropetalum is a superb addition to home landscapes. The evergreen leaves and crooked, downy stems of this midsized shrub are its outstanding features for most of the year. For several weeks in spring, however, the soft-looking foliage is overshadowed by countless creamy white, silken tufts of flowers similar to witch hazel blossoms but even showier. After this heavy spring bloom, flower clusters continue to appear at leaf nodes throughout the year.

Loropetalum has a compact though irregular growth habit that gives it great character. Branches droop lightly, holding the pale green foliage in even tiers. Growth is fast to 3 feet, then slows as it matures to 5 feet tall. Some specimens develop broad, twisted forms; others are more upright, and still others have long, arching branches.

HOW TO GROW

Like most other members of the witch hazel family, loropetalum needs moist, well-drained, acidic soil that is rich in organic matter. It does not tolerate alkaline soils. Some shade is best, although in cool climates, it grows well in part sun. In Zone 6, loropetalum may die back to the ground without winter protection, but it will resprout in spring.

LANDSCAPE USE

Loropetalum is an excellent specimen shrub for a raised planter. Elevating the branches to eye level brings the crooked stems, textured leaves, and delicate, fragrant flowers into easy view. Place it in the foreground of a shrub border for close-up viewing; positioned farther away, the delicate blossoms become an indistinct, cloudy haze. Take advantage of the dense foliage and use it to shield the open, leggy growth of other, taller background shrubs.

Top Choices

- *L.* 'Burgundy' has evergreen leaves with undertones of burgundy. Spectacular and fragrant, its deep pink flowers bloom in spring followed by scattered blossoms through summer.

- *L.* 'Snow Dance' has compact, 2-foot stems with evergreen leaves and snow white flowers in spring.

LOROPETALUM FOR NATURAL GARDENS

Consider loropetalum for a massed woodland planting with other shade-loving shrubs. The pale and delicate foliage pairs well with more coarsely textured rhododendrons and mountain laurel (*Kalmia latifolia*), witch hazel (*Hamamelis* spp.), and winter hazel (*Corylopsis* spp.). It also looks beautiful when underplanted with ferns and candelabra primroses.

TO PRUNE OR NOT TO PRUNE

This shrub is most handsome when allowed to develop its natural, irregular, rounded shape, though it can be pruned if it grows out of bounds. It recovers quickly from clipping or from deep rejuvenation pruning. It can be limbed up from the bottom to expose its rich brown, exfoliating bark, a treatment particularly useful in oriental gardens.

SIBERIAN CARPET CYPRESS
Microbiota decussata

Zones: 2–9

Type: Evergreen

Light: Sun or shade

Size: 1–2 ft. tall,
5–8 ft. wide or more

Uses: Ground cover,
mass planting, rock
garden

Interest: Evergreen
foliage

Siberian carpet cypress is a relatively new coniferous shrub in American gardens. Its scalelike foliage is similar to arborvitae, but its spreading form is more suggestive of low-growing junipers. Unlike many other conifers, it thrives in shade as well as in sun. Considered a dwarf because of its low-growing habit, Siberian carpet cypress spreads quickly with bright green sprays of long, finely leaved branches. Siberian carpet cypress is evergreen and extremely cold hardy; its winter foliage develops reddish purple tints if grown in sun.

HOW TO GROW
An undemanding plant, Siberian carpet cypress thrives in ordinary, even harsh, conditions. Loose, well-drained, slightly acidic to neutral soil is best. Drought-tolerant once established, the plants should be watered regularly

after planting and through the first summer. In a mostly sunny or slightly shaded site, Siberian carpet cypress will quickly spread to 5 feet wide or more. Feathery and graceful, it requires virtually no maintenance. When planting several of this shrub as a ground cover, mulch between plants to discourage weeds until branches provide a dense cover. The horizontal stems will layer naturally, producing new plants.

LANDSCAPE USE

This lacy little shrub provides year-round interest, contrasting with the geometrical shapes of sheared yews and boxwoods. Like other dwarf conifers, Siberian carpet cypress can be a striking feature as a specimen in a rock garden or in a low island bed. Planted near ponds or water gardens, its feathery texture is a picturesque contrast to bold wetland plants.

The low profile of Siberian carpet cypress accents taller landscape plants. In a small urban garden or patio, it assumes a central role as an understory plant or as a trailing ground cover under a small, limbed-up tree. In cold climates, its dense growth is effective on banks with plants set 4 to 5 feet apart, or at the top of a retaining wall where it will gracefully drape over the edge.

Top Choice

• *M.* 'Vancouver' reaches 8 to 12 inches tall with feathery, dark green foliage that turns greenish purple in winter. It is more vigorous than the species.

LOW-GROWING CONIFERS

Most conifers tend to grow upright, many to soaring heights. Low-growing forms are sometimes miniature versions of their larger relatives, or are plants that have evolved a low-growing habit in response to their natural environment.

An example of the latter is Siberian carpet cypress. It was discovered in the 1920s growing above the timberline in the Siberian mountains. It is one of a select few low-growing conifers that thrive in extreme conditions. This hardiness, coupled with a creeping habit and feathery foliage, make it a better choice and value than many other more popular low-growing conifers.

Other hardy creeping conifers, such as shore juniper and creeping juniper, make excellent companions to Siberian carpet cypress, creating a beautiful evergreen tapestry.

BAYBERRY
Myrica pensylvanica

Zones: 3–8

Type: Deciduous to semi-evergreen

Light: Full to part sun

Size: 8–10 ft. tall, 8–10 ft. wide

Uses: Hedge, mass planting, seaside garden, wildlife garden

Interest: Aromatic foliage; berries in summer through winter

Bayberry is valued as much for its homey scent as for its shiny, thick foliage and its dependability in northern climates. Dark green, leathery leaves and waxy berries contain aromatic oils that release a pleasant fragrance when crushed. Leaves develop little fall color, remaining green well into autumn. In winter, blue-gray, waxy berries cling closely to branches and stems on the previous season's wood.

HOW TO GROW
Plant bayberry in full to part sun. It does best and grows fastest in sandy, acidic soil, but it is very tolerant and adapts to clay and ordinary conditions. Alkaline soils can cause yellow spots (chlorosis) to develop on leaves. Remedy by amending the soil to lower pH. For a temporary fix, apply a spray of chelated iron to the foliage.

Bayberry requires little maintenance. It responds well to pruning to even out widely spaced branches and control its shape. Unpruned, its natural contours give it a rounded, rugged character all its own. Bayberry spreads by underground stolons; it is best used in naturalistic settings.

LANDSCAPE USE

Native to seaside habitats, bayberry thrives in coastal landscapes, tolerating salt spray and adverse conditions while developing a windswept look. Inland, plants grow taller with a more refined shape. Medium- to fast-growing, bayberry can be planted alone or in groups; it can be clipped or left unpruned. Use it for hedges, foundation plants, or alone as a foliage accent. Its habit of suckering also makes it useful for controlling erosion on slopes. Space individual plants 8 to 10 feet apart for mass plantings or hedges.

Bayberry's low maintenance requirements and hardy nature make it a good choice for native landscapes and wildlife gardens. It works well with other native or naturalized plants in meadows or along the edge of a pond.

Top Choice

- *M. gale*, sweet gale, is a close relative of bayberry that thrives in wet, boggy sites. The compact, 3-foot-tall, trouble-free plants have glossy, dark green, very aromatic leaves.

WARM-CLIMATE BAYBERRIES

Pacific wax myrtle, *M. californica*, is a West Coast native hardy in Zones 7 to 10. It also bears glossy, dark green, willowlike foliage and berries that attract birds. Growing to 30 feet tall, it makes a good hedge, screen, or specimen.

Pacific wax myrtle does best along the coast with high shade and ocean fog; it needs more shade inland. Once established, it is quite adaptive and drought-tolerant. Use it in landscapes as a large shrub or trained as a small tree.

Southern wax myrtle, *M. cerifera*, is a graceful accent and hedge plant. Its grayish white bark is quite handsome when lower branches are removed to give it a tree form. Two varieties are 'Fairfax', which grows 4 to 5 feet tall, and 'Georgia Gem', which has smaller, lighter leaves and stays below 2 feet. Zones 7 to 9.

ENSURING BERRIES

The bluish gray, waxy-coated bayberry fruit clusters are used to scent bayberry candles. Berries are produced only on female plants. To ensure fruit, you must have a male plant nearby.

NANDINA
Nandina domestica

Zones: 6–9

Type: Evergreen

Light: Sun to shade

Size: 6–8 ft. tall,
2–3 ft. wide

Uses: Hedge, ground
cover (dwarf forms),
mass planting, rock
garden, shrub border

Interest: Spring flow-
ers; fall berries

Nandina, or heavenly bamboo, is a tough, depend-able plant that thrives in difficult conditions and provides a rainbow of cheerful colors. Deeply divided leaves and pointed leaflets give it a lacy, feathery look. New foliage emerges pink to copper, then turns bluish or pale green. Some varieties develop a rich red color in summer; others wait for cooler weather to unveil their crimson tones. White flower panicles in late spring yield bright red ornamental berries by fall. Other varieties are treated with a harmless virus to induce crinkling and produce colorful yellowish green-and-red foliage.

HOW TO GROW
Plant nandina in rich soil in a sunny site for the most intense foliage color. Once established, it needs no fur-ther attention and can survive the driest summers.

With average care, it will slowly expand by underground rhizomes and develop into a clump.

LANDSCAPE USE

One of nandina's greatest attributes is its ability to fit into narrow spaces where few other plants are appropriate. Its vertical canes and leafy horizontal tiers are perfect for niches near buildings, as foils around posts, and in narrow planting strips. Plant tall varieties 2 to 3 feet away from solid walls and fences so the canes have ample room to arch gracefully. When planting under trees, set nandina in open beds. Plant a low-growing ground cover under tall varieties.

Among its other virtues, heavenly bamboo successfully competes with tree roots. Dwarf varieties are best for rock gardens, containers, and ground covers. Tall varieties of fast-growing heavenly bamboo make open, airy hedges and add interesting textural contrasts when planted among conifers. This shrub is indispensable in an oriental garden.

Top Choices

- N. 'Alba' has antique white berries with yellow fall color. Plants reach 6 feet tall.
- N. 'Moyers Red', a good variety for the South, grows 5 to 6 feet tall. Its pink flowers and red fruit are followed by reddish purple winter foliage.

NANDINA FOR SMALL SPACES

Dwarf varieties are low and compact and seem to thrive on neglect. In the right location, they require no attention after planting.

- *N.* 'Fire Power' grows 1 to 2 feet tall and 2 feet wide. It has bold red winter color.
- *N.* 'Gulf Stream' is a compact, 2- to 3-foot tall variety with bluish green to bright red leaves.
- *N.* 'Harbor Dwarf' forms compact, 2-foot-tall clumps and turns reddish purple in winter.
- *N.* 'Nana Purpurea' grows 1 to 2 feet tall with coarse, closely set, reddish purple foliage.
- *N.* 'Wood's Dwarf' is a very compact, 1- to 2-foot-tall variety with beautiful orange to crimson fall color.

MOCK ORANGE
Philadelphus coronarius

Zones: 4–8

Type: Deciduous

Light: Full to part sun

Size: 10 ft. tall,
10 ft. wide

Uses: Shrub border,
specimen

Interest: Fragrant early-
summer flowers

Few floral delights are as sweet as the orange-blossom fragrance of mock orange in bloom. The plants bear exquisite, snow-white blossoms decorated with a central brush of yellow stamens. This sentimental favorite has been grown in gardens alongside bridal-wreath spirea and peegee hydrangea since Victorian times. Mock orange is a large shrub with multiple stems, often reaching surprising heights. Kept in check, it is a welcome addition to the garden.

HOW TO GROW
Mock orange thrives in ordinary soil with good drainage and at least a half day of sun. Locate it in a site large enough to handle its extensive root system. Though mock orange is easy to grow, it is not maintenance-free. Prune annually after bloom to control its vigorous, often

leggy growth. Remove the oldest and weakest stems at the base to encourage new shoots and a more abundant future bloom. Plants used as background shrubs and corner plantings look best when some of the tall stems are retained. Cut some of these tall branches back every other year.

LANDSCAPE USE

Dwarf forms of mock orange, such as 'Miniature Snowflake' and 'Avalanche', have a fuller, tidier appearance than the species. Locate these shrubs in areas where the flowers' enchanting fragrance can be best enjoyed. Mock orange has been a standard of all-white (moon) gardens for generations. Include several varieties for a framework with staggered bloom times.

Top Choices

- *P.* 'Avalanche' grows to 4 feet tall with drooping stems loaded with white, extremely fragrant, single blossoms.

- *P.* 'Buckley's Quill' is a semidwarf that grows 6 feet tall and 4 feet wide. Flowers have abundant, quill-shaped white petals.

- *P.* 'Miniature Snowflake' is a compact 3-foot variety that grows to the same width. This beautiful variety has deep green, disease-resistant foliage and abundant, very fragrant double blossoms in summer.

RENEWING MOCK ORANGE

When neglected, mock oranges become an impenetrable thicket of leggy, upright, woody stems. To renew a shrub and restore its appearance:

1 Remove one-third of the oldest canes as close to the base as possible to make way for strong new growth.

2 The following year, remove half of the remaining oldest canes; remove the balance the third year.

3 Thereafter, continue to cut out some of the oldest canes every year after flowering.

In addition to pruning, mock orange can be invigorated by dividing every five years:

1 Use a shovel to root-prune around the clump, and then lift the plant from the soil with a garden fork.

2 Shake off excess soil and chop the clump into two or three sections with a hatchet or sharp shovel blade. Plant divisions immediately.

ANDROMEDA
Pieris japonica

Zones: 5–8

Type: Evergreen

Light: Part sun

Size: 9–12 ft. tall, 6–8 ft. wide

Uses: Shrub border, specimen, woodland planting

Interest: Evergreen foliage; spring flowers; colorful new foliage

Andromeda, or Japanese pieris, is an elegant evergreen plant with handsome springtime flowers. Its small, creamy white blossoms look like clusters of delicate bells and have a light scent sought out by early-season bumblebees. Erect branches display the leathery green foliage in neat, horizontal tiers. Spring growth, in shades of pink and reddish bronze, deepens to lustrous, glossy green in summer. Flower buds form along the stems during summer and autumn, opening in winter in mild climates and early spring elsewhere.

HOW TO GROW
Like many of its woodland companions such as mountain laurel and rhododendron, Japanese pieris requires ample water and shelter from drying sun and wind. Plant it in part sun in cool climates and in afternoon

shade where summers are hot. It prefers acidic, fertile loam yet does well in average soil amended with peat moss or leaf mold to provide organic matter and good drainage. It does not tolerate severe dryness, high alkalinity, or wet soil.

Fertilize Japanese pieris in spring and early summer, especially in areas of high rainfall. Keep the root zone mulched with several inches of bark chips or pine needles. Deadhead faded blossoms to prevent the formation of unattractive seedpods.

LANDSCAPE USE

Japanese pieris is most attractive in plantings that are not crowded, displaying the shrub's lovely silhouette and foliage. Near a house, it adds an elegant touch when combined with conifers and evergreen holly. In shrub borders and low beds, the deep green foliage is a refined accent. Few plants are so useful for brightening dull corners and shaded paths. Its graceful contours become more beautiful as the plant ages.

Japanese pieris is an ideal companion for rhododendrons and mountain laurels, and it blends equally well with other woodland denizens. Choose from dozens of cultivars of this shrub for blossom and foliage color, vigor, and compactness.

Top Choice

- P. 'Mountain Fire' grows to 6 feet tall with bright red new growth that provides a bold accent to the spring landscape. As the leaves mature, they turn a rich emerald green. Flowers are white and fragrant.

MORE ANDROMEDAS

Mountain andromeda, *Pieris floribunda,* is native to the Appalachian Mountains and is hardy from Zones 4 to 7. The plants grow 4 to 6 feet tall with a mounded habit and lustrous tiers of evergreen leaves. New growth has bronze tones and emerges after the clusters of fragrant white flowers. 'Brouwer's Beauty', a hybrid between *Pieris floribunda* and *Pieris japonica*, is one of the finest of all andromeda varieties. The plants grow 3 to 6 feet tall with dark green leaves, a neat and compact habit, and deep burgundy red flower buds that open to reveal long-lasting white flowers. The new foliage is yellow-green and quite attractive.

CONTROLLING LACE BUGS

Lace bugs are tiny insects that may cause serious damage to Japanese pieris in the eastern part of the country. Difficult to control, these bugs suck juices from leaves, peppering the foliage with yellow and brown spots. Severe infestations can cause defoliation. Control by cutting out damaged foliage and spray every two weeks with insecticidal soap.

BUSH CINQUEFOIL
Potentilla fruticosa

Zones: 2–7

Type: Deciduous

Light: Full sun

Size: 2–3 ft. tall,
3–4 ft. wide

Uses: Mass planting,
shrub or perennial bor-
der, rock garden

Interest: Summer
flowers

Bush cinquefoil is one of those all-purpose, small shrubs that has a place in nearly every cold-climate garden. Native to northern latitudes and mountainous regions, it is most at home in areas with cold winters and does not do well south of Zone 7. Small yellow, pink, or white cupped flowers resembling wild roses are bush cinquefoil's greatest charm. They appear all summer long with the heaviest bloom in early summer. Most varieties are densely bushy and multi-branched with spreading stems; others have a more upright habit.

HOW TO GROW
Bush cinquefoil does best in a sunny, well-drained site with fertile clay or loamy soil. It tolerates many conditions, including compacted and sandy soils. Fertilizing is required only for plants grown in containers and those

grown in poor soil. Flower production is heaviest and the shape more regular when one-third of the oldest stems are cut to the ground each winter. Use this technique to restore flowering to older, unpruned plants.

LANDSCAPE USE

This remarkably versatile plant fits easily into mixed perennial or shrub borders. In rock gardens, pair bush cinquefoil with creeping ground covers, low-growing mugho pines, and ornamental grasses. It looks charming along a picket fence among perennials or as a low, lightly clipped hedge. Bush cinquefoil's neat, trim appearance makes it ideal for small urban gardens. It can even be planted in containers to set on decks and patios.

A member of the rose family, bush cinquefoil is also an excellent companion for a multitude of roses. It makes a lovely complement to a background of colorful summer climbers or to a rugosa rose covered with vibrant orange hips in fall.

Top Choices

- *P.* 'Abbotswood' reaches 4 feet tall and 6 feet wide with snow white flowers and dark greenish blue foliage.

- *P.* 'Gold Drop' grows 2 feet tall with deep yellow flowers all summer.

- *P.* 'Pink Beauty' has pale pink blossoms on compact 2-foot-tall plants.

- *P.* 'Sunset' bears rich golden orange flowers on 1-foot-tall plants.

PLANTING IN CONTAINERS

Bush cinquefoil thrives in containers. After purchasing a container-grown plant from your local nursery, gently separate the plant from the pot.

1 Place a few inches of potting soil in the bottom of a slightly larger pot; place the shrub in the new container.

2 Fill around the rootball with potting soil, firming the soil gently and watering well.

3 In fall, after a few hard frosts, place the container in an unheated garage or basement. Loosely cover the plants with white plastic and water when the soil is dry, taking care not to overwater.

PATIENCE PAYS

Bush cinquefoil can be late to leaf out in spring. Be patient and wait for buds to break before cutting back stems that appear winter-damaged. After spring growth begins, dead twigs will be apparent and can be removed.

FIRE THORN

Pyracantha spp.

Zones: 6–9 and milder parts of Zone 5

Type: Semi-evergreen

Light: Full sun to part shade

Size: 8–10 ft. tall, 10–20 ft. wide

Uses: Barrier hedge, espalier, shrub border

Interest: Colorful fall berries; long-lasting foliage

Fire thorn's plentiful, very ornamental red berries make it one of the best shrubs for fall and early-winter color. When plants are grown close together, the thorny, irregular branches also make a useful barrier hedge. In late spring, clusters of creamy white flowers dangle on spurs along the branches of the previous year's growth. Though visually attractive, the blossoms have a somewhat unpleasant odor.

HOW TO GROW

Fire thorn tolerates a wide range of growing conditions, with the exception of highly alkaline or soggy soil. Plants that receive a balanced fertilizer in midspring and are kept evenly moist perform best. When well established, they can endure high heat and long periods of drought. Plant container-grown or balled-and-burlapped fire thorns in early spring. Locate plants in full sun for the best crops of flowers and fruits. When grown in part shade, firethorn produces fewer flowers and berries.

Rambling, free-growing plants are excellent for out-of-the-way sites. Lightly sheared fire thorns make a great informal hedge. Cut back frost-damaged shoots in early spring and trim out any wayward branches. If fire blight causes dieback at the tips, cut affected branches 6 to 12 inches below the diseased area. To avoid spreading this disease, be sure to disinfect your pruning shears with bleach after each cut.

LANDSCAPE USE

The dense growth of fire thorn can be trimmed into a hedge or allowed to branch freely as a screen or barrier. Locate plants where their spectacular show of fiery berries can best be appreciated in fall and early winter. Fire thorn is one of the best plants to use for an espalier. It can easily be shaped into interesting patterns on a fence or wall to display its blossoms and profuse fruits. The ornamental berries on 'Apache' and 'Mohave' are not eaten by birds and so remain on plants for several months.

Top Choices

- *P.* 'Apache' has dark, glossy green leaves and bright scarlet berries.

- *P.* 'Mohave' bears abundant flowers and loads of bright orange berries.

- *P.* 'Teton' has an upright habit and yellow-orange fruit.

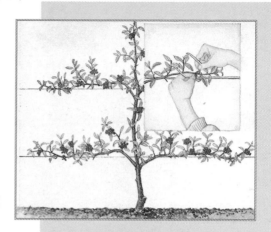

CREATING AN ESPALIER

With repeated pruning, you can create a simple or dramatic espalier along a blank wall or fence. This is a a valuable technique to use in small gardens and patios. Train branches to grow in parallel horizontal rows, in a fan or candelabra shape, or in a diamond pattern or other geometric design.

❶ In spring or early summer, tie low branches of a young, flexible plant onto secure horizontal supporting wires.

❷ Cut back vertical shoots to a bud that is 1 to 2 inches from the base. Remove shoots growing into or away from the wall.

❸ Tie the central leader to a vertical wire, or cut it off below a parallel wire to stimulate new growth of horizontal branches.

AZALEA
Rhododendron spp.

Zones: Varies by group

Type: Deciduous to evergreen

Light: Full to part sun

Size: Size varies

Uses: Container or foundation plant, shrub border, mass planting

Interest: Spring flowers; handsome foliage

Azaleas, which are members of the *Rhododendron* genus, are perhaps the most decorative and varied of all flowering shrubs. They may be deciduous or evergreen and their colors range from delicate whites and pastels to vivid oranges and reds. The Gable hybrids pictured above are among the hardiest of the evergreen azaleas (Zones 6 to 9; with protection to Zone 5). In spring, the plants are covered with spectacular 2-inch blossoms in a variety of flaming colors. If possible, buy azaleas in bloom from a local nursery for the best selection of color and hardiness.

HOW TO GROW
Azaleas grow well in most of the country except the Southwest and Plains. They require loose, light, acidic soil with lots of organic matter to help hold moisture.

Amend with prodigious amounts of acidic organic matter—peat moss or shredded oak leaves.

Plant azaleas with the top of the rootball slightly above the soil level, then cover with a thick mulch. Replenish the mulch as needed and avoid cultivating near the shallow roots. Provide extra water during dry spells. Once established, apply a time-release, acidifying fertilizer in spring when flower buds first show color.

LANDSCAPE USE

Azaleas add a sophisticated look to homes and gardens. Plant them along foundations or in shrub borders. Mass plantings are dramatic in spring. Small forms make wonderful container plants.

Top Choices

- Gable hybrids have dark green leaves and large flowers. Zones 5 to 9.

- Glen Dale hybrids have large blossoms but are hardy from Zones 6 to 9.

- Kurume hybrids are compact, 4-foot-tall plants with glossy, evergreen leaves and heavy spring bloom. Zones 7 to 9.

- North Tisbury hybrids have a trailing form with large flowers. Zones 6 to 9.

- Robin Hill hybrids have large, pastel-colored flowers on compact, spreading plants. Zones 6 to 9.

- Southern Indica hybrids have large flowers and are excellent container plants. Zones 8 to 10.

Taylor's Tips

PROMOTING BUSHINESS

To stimulate bushiness and increased flower production the following spring, pinch the tips of new growth after flowering, removing the terminal bud.

Cut back leggy plants by making a pruning cut at any point along the stem. New shoots will emerge from dormant buds just below the cut along the stems.

DECIDUOUS AZALEAS

Deciduous hybrid azaleas are hardy shrubs with heavy blooms of showy flowers in spring. Many are hardy in Zone 5, and some flower reliably in Zone 4. The soft green summer foliage turns shades of orange, red, and purple in fall.

- The Knap Hill and Exbury groups grow 4 to 8 feet tall with large, often fragrant flowers. The blossoms come in many colors.

- Northern Lights is a group of hybrids hardy to Zone 3. The plants grow 6 feet tall with fragrant flowers in shades of white, rose-red, pink, yellow, and orange.

YAKU RHODODENDRON
Rhododendron yakusimanum

Zones: 5–9

Type: Evergreen

Light: Part shade

Size: 3–5 ft. tall,
5 ft. wide

Uses: Shrub border,
mass planting,
specimen

Interest: Spring flow-
ers; evergreen foliage

Yaku rhododendron and its cultivars, most often called yaks, are handsome plants with new leaves covered with soft fuzz and older foliage turning a shiny, dark green. They are cherished for their compact size, dense branching structure, and delicate blossoms. The bell-shaped, 2- to 3-inch flowers begin as deep pink buds that fade to apple-blossom white. These appear in midspring in immense trusses up to 9 inches across.

HOW TO GROW

All rhododendrons and azaleas share the same cultural needs. When they struggle in the landscape, it is most often due to inadequate organic material, improper soil pH, or poor drainage. Rhododendrons need a loose, acidic, humus-rich soil. In heavy clay or dry sandy soil, the roots will not prosper.

At planting time, loosen roots of container-grown plants with a hand cultivator, or slit the outside of the rootball on four sides. Spread roots out as far as possible. Set the plant so the top of the rootball is slightly higher than the surrounding soil. Top with several inches of organic mulch. Avoid cultivating near the shrub's roots and always keep the soil moist.

LANDSCAPE USE

Evergreen Yaku rhododendron is a very reliable, all-season shrub. 'Yaku Princess' is one of the most attractive cultivars. It makes an excellent foundation shrub or understory plant with dogwoods and Japanese maples. 'Mist Maiden' is more vigorous and has striking foliage.

Top Choices

The following choices are other evergreen rhododendrons grouped by blossom color with height and hardiness following the cultivar name:

- Red: 'Holden', 4 ft., Zones 4 to 9; 'Jean Marie De Montague', 5 ft., Zones 5 to 8; 'Nova Zembla', 5 ft., Zones 5 to 9.

- Lavender/purple: 'English Roseum' and 'Roseum Elegans', 8 ft., Zones 5 to 8; 'P. J. M.', 6 ft., Zones 4 to 8.

- White: 'Anna H. Hall', 4 ft., Zones 5 to 9; 'Boule de Neige', 5 ft., Zones 5 to 9; 'Cunningham's White', 4 ft., Zones 5 to 9.

- Pink: 'Bali', 3 ft., Zones 5 to 8; 'Janet Blair', 6 ft., Zones 5 to 8; 'Pink Dawn', 6 ft., Zones 4 to 8; 'Scintillation', 5 ft., Zones 5 to 8; 'Waltham', 2 ft., Zones 5 to 8.

DEADHEADING FADED BLOSSOMS

When rhododendrons are planted in full view and in small enough numbers, their appearance is greatly enhanced by removing the dead flower heads.

While other shrubs can be deadheaded by a quick overall shearing or by indiscriminately clipping off stem tips, rhododendrons require careful attention in order to avoid damaging the new shoots.

To remove faded flower clusters, cut them from the stem with a small pair of clippers or use your fingertips, taking care not to disturb the brittle shoots.

ALPINE CURRANT

Ribes alpinum

Zones: 3–7

Type: Deciduous

Light: Full sun to part shade

Size: 3–6 ft. tall, 3–6 ft. wide

Uses: Barrier hedge, foundation or mass planting

Interest: Attractive stems; colorful fall foliage

Alpine currant is one of the best foliage plants for difficult conditions, particularly in northern climates. Its ridged stems of shiny brown are quite attractive in winter. In spring, the bright green leaves are among the earliest to leaf out, bringing a fresh look to a faded landscape. The dense foliage obscures the small, greenish yellow, springtime flowers. Choose male plants, which do not bear fruit, because they are immune to rust diseases.

HOW TO GROW

Ornamental alpine currants are easy to grow. They thrive in full sun or deep shade and everything in between, including a wide variety of soil conditions. Take extra precautions at planting time, providing good drainage to avoid root rot in wet soil.

Set hedge plants 3 feet apart. At a greater distance, this mostly upright plant will be slow to fill in. With maturity, the hedge will be compact and naturally rounded, and it will respond to any degree of pruning. It is attractive sheared or unsheared.

LANDSCAPE USE

The naturally dense, round shape and the small foliage of alpine currant make it a choice shrub for planting in groups or alone as a foundation plant. It works well at corners where its broad size has room to develop. Alpine currant, with its dense branching and thick foliage, is one of the best plants for hedges. Unpruned, it makes a relaxed but tidy barrier hedge or low screen. Trimmed, the plants lend a formal appearance to gardens and borders.

CAUTION: Alpine currants, the species used in landscaping, are different from those planted for fruit. Some types of currants used for fruit production are banned from interstate commerce due to the possibility that they may spread white pine blister rust, a serious disease of white pines. Alpine currant plants are not affected by these restrictions.

Top Choices

- *R.* 'Aureum' grows to 3 feet tall with yellowish green leaves. Site the plants in full sun for best foliage color.

- *R.* 'Green Mound' is a dwarf variety growing 2 to 3 feet tall with dark green leaves and a dense, compact habit. It is a fine choice for a low hedge. Foliage turns golden yellow in fall.

SHAPING A HEDGE

A hedge develops the most density when the sides are tapered, with the top narrower than the bottom. Keeping the top narrow allows more light to reach the foliage and, in cold zones, protects against damaging weight from heavy snow. Flat hedges are most common, but you may want to consider a pyramid, arch, or rounded dome to cap the top.

- Trim hedge plants gradually as they mature to encourage bushiness. Waiting until the ideal height is reached results in a sparsely filled shrub.

- Shear a mature hedge only as needed (as infrequently as possible), since pruning stimulates growth. Shear harder and more frequently to restore a weak hedge. For straight cuts, set up sight lines with string and stakes.

- Alpine currant develops dense, twiggy growth naturally. Shearing encourages its normal habit. Make cuts with a well-sharpened tool beginning in late spring after growth starts; repeat in midsummer. If growth is slow, one summer pruning may be sufficient.

SKIMMIA
Skimmia japonica

Zones: 7–9

Type: Evergreen

Light: Part to full shade

Size: 3–5 ft. tall, 3–5 ft. wide

Uses: Foundation or mass planting, shrub border

Interest: Aromatic, evergreen foliage; fragrant spring flowers; red berries in fall

Skimmia is a neat, compact, evergreen shrub that adds several decorative elements to gardens in mild-winter climates. In spring, fragrant white flowers in 2- to 3-inch domed clusters stand on reddish stems above tidy, glossy leaves. In fall, new buds take on a striking red tint that holds through winter along with the decorative clusters of dangling red berries. These hollylike fruits are often still on the shrub as blossoms open the following spring. Skimmia's shiny, sometimes wavy leaves have the scent of sweet bay when crushed. Avoid handling the attractive, but poisonous, berries.

HOW TO GROW
Grow skimmia in part to full shade in moist, humus-rich, slightly acidic soil. If drainage is questionable in heavy soil, plant in raised beds or use in large planter

boxes. Take careful note of the exposure at planting time to avoid placing this shrub on south-facing slopes where it can receive damaging direct winter sun. Slow-growing skimmia develops a compact habit without pruning. In alkaline soils, add peat moss to the soil at planting time. Maintain proper pH around established plants by applying an acidifying fertilizer after flowering is complete. Over a period of several years, cut back the oldest stems to within 4 inches of the ground to maintain the shrubs' vigor.

LANDSCAPE USE

Individual skimmia plants vary somewhat in height and spread, but all are well behaved and good-looking for years on end. This species is an ideal foundation plant or freestanding shrub in small gardens. Its intimate size makes it a good border plant along sidewalks and entryways. It is also effective in raised beds or large containers. Planted in drifts, the smooth layers of foliage create a uniform expanse of green.

Top Choices

- *S.* x *formanii* has dark green leaves and white flowers that yield abundant clusters of red fruit. It requires a male variety nearby to set fruit.

- *S.* 'Nymans' is a female variety with dark green leaves. Its bright red berries are larger than those of other varieties. It will produce a very heavy crop of berries but only if a male variety is planted nearby.

Taylor's Tips

PLANTING FOR POLLINATION

Male skimmias are more shapely and produce showier blossoms, but only the female plants bear fruit. If you want berries to form on your skimmia, allow space for two plants, one male and one female.

For mass plantings, be sure to provide a male pollinator for every six females. 'Bronze Knight' and 'Rubella' are male varieties with showy red flower buds and stems. 'Macrophylla' is a large-leaved male variety.

USING SKIMMIA IN SHADY PLACES

Like other shade-loving plants, skimmia is well suited to woodland plantings. It fits easily with other understory plants such as enkianthus and witch hazel.

JAPANESE SPIREA
Spiraea japonica var. *alpina*

Zones: 3–9

Type: Deciduous

Light: Full to part sun

Size: 2–3 ft. tall,
2–3 ft. wide

Uses: Beds and borders, container plant, foundation planting

Interest: Summer flowers; colorful fall foliage

One of the smallest of the spireas, *Spirea japonica* var. *alpina* is a fine-textured, mounding shrub that grows wider than it does tall. This diminutive variety is smaller and more dainty than its more popular relatives that have become something of an institution in American gardens. This delicate little shrub bears pincushion-domed flowers that are unmistakably spirea. From late spring to early summer, Japanese spirea is covered with dainty pink blossoms that nearly hide its dense foliage. In fall, its leaves turn to muted shades of orange and red.

HOW TO GROW
Japanese spirea's basic needs are easy to satisfy, as the plant is content with average, slightly acidic soil and moderate water. Spirea tolerates both wind and drought

and grows well in full sun or light shade, though flowering is heaviest in sun. In neutral to alkaline soil, the foliage turns yellow. Apply iron chelate as a temporary remedy while you adjust the soil pH. Like all spireas, this miniature shrub benefits from having the oldest stems cut back to the ground every few years. Prune branch ends in very early spring to induce fullness. After flowering, trim off faded blooms.

LANDSCAPE USE

Japanese spirea is one of the most versatile of the spireas. Its low habit makes it useful for massing as a small-area ground cover around larger shrubs and under small trees. Repeated several times in a mixed border, it can serve as a unifying element among mid-sized shrubs and perennials. Use this low-growing spirea to spill out from a shaded bank of hostas onto a sunny slope or to cascade over a retaining wall, a raised bed, or a series of terraces. Plant several as a bulb cover to surround late-blooming tulips. The shrub's small size makes it a natural for urban gardens where space is scarce.

Top Choices

- S. 'Candle Light' has pale yellow foliage and light pink flowers.
- S. 'Everblooming' bears pink flowers from summer to fall.
- S. 'Neon Flash' has red blossoms and pinkish red new growth.

Taylor's Tips

SUMMER-FLOWERING SPIREAS

Bumald spireas (S. x bumalda) are lovely deciduous hybrids that grow 2 to 3 feet tall and bloom in white to deep pink. These hardy plants are widely grown in Zones 3 to 9.

- Ever-popular 'Anthony Waterer' has rosy pink flowers with foliage tinged pink in spring and purplish red in fall.
- 'Crispa' has crinkled leaves and light pink flowers.
- The foliage of 'Gold Flame' provides a kaleidoscope of color —from gold to chartreuse, yellow, and orange—through three seasons.

NAMED VARIETIES

Since much confusion exists in identifying many spirea cultivars, you may find *Spiraea japonica* var. *alpina* under the name 'Nana' or 'Nyewoods'. 'Little Princess' is deeper pink and taller than Japanese spirea. A similar variety, 'Shibori' (syn. 'Shirobana'), bears pink, white, and red flowers on the same plant.

LILAC

Syringa spp.

Zones: 2–8 (varies by species)

Type: Deciduous

Light: Full to part sun

Size: Varies by species

Uses: Informal hedge, shrub border, specimen

Interest: Fragrant flowers

Lilacs are loved for their glorious scent and colorful blossoms. They appear in the landscape for nostalgia as much as for utility, since they are most attractive when in bloom. Out of flower, they blend unpretentiously into the background, offering deep green foliage that mixes well in borders with summer-flowering shrubs. Planting early- and late-blooming species ensures a fragrant and colorful show for many weeks during spring.

HOW TO GROW

Add lime to acidic soils for lilacs and place them where they will receive at least 6 hours of sun a day. As the plants grow, pinch the tips to promote bushiness and flowering potential. To deadhead clusters after bloom for improved air circulation and heavier flowering next year, cut below the flower stem and just above a pair of buds. Flowers will form during the summer for next year's blooms. Thin out weak new growth and the oldest, woodiest stems after several years to renew vigor from the ground up. Many lilacs are prone to powdery mildew in late summer; it covers the leaves with an unattractive whitish fuzz but does little harm.

LANDSCAPE USE

Different lilacs accent the landscape in different ways. The Canadian hybrids and common lilac are best used in shrub borders or as an informal hedge. *S. patula* 'Miss Kim', with dainty clusters of small, very fragrant flowers, is useful as a foundation plant.

Top Choices

- *S. patula* 'Miss Kim' has late-blooming lilac flowers and a tidy, compact habit. It thrives in warm and cold regions. Plants grow 4 to 8 feet tall, with mildew-resistant foliage that turns red in fall. Zones 4 to 8.

- *S. x prestoniae*, Canadian hybrids, are very hardy and bloom at a younger age than most lilacs. 'Hiawatha' has pale pink flowers and 'Nocturne' bears lavender flowers. Zones 3 to 7.

- *S. vulgaris*, common lilac, includes: 'Miss Ellen Willmot' and 'Mont Blanc' (white), 'President Grevy' and 'President Lincoln' (blue), 'Belle de Nancy' and 'Lucie Baltet' (pink), 'Charles Joly' and 'Congo' (burgundy), 'Sarah Sands' and 'Zulu' (violet), and 'Primrose' (yellow). Zones 3 to 7.

Taylor's Tips

HEAVENLY SCENTS

Some of the sweetest lilac perfumes come from single and light-colored varieties on 1- to 2-inch stems, often after cool, rainy springs. Two especially fragrant *S. vulgaris* varieties with double florets are creamy white 'Krasavitsa Moskvy' (Beauty of Moscow) and 'Miss Ellen Willmott'. The latter has perhaps the very best blooms of all the white lilacs; it is also nonsuckering.

ALL FOR SHOW

One of the showiest lilacs is tall-growing Japanese tree lilac, *S. reticulata*. Best in northern gardens, its airy flower panicles lack lilac's traditional scent. It relies instead on its translucent, mahogany-red bark to stop the show. This lilac makes an excellent specimen or street tree. Zones 3 to 7.

YEW

Taxus

Zones: 2–8

Type: Evergreen

Light: Full sun to full shade

Size: Varies by type

Uses: Formal hedge, foundation planting, screen

Interest: Evergreen foliage

Yews, best known as hedge shrubs, bestow a refined, formal look to ordinary landscapes. These variable plants, some of which grow only a few inches a year while others grow larger and faster, are easily trimmed into many compact geometric shapes. The short, flat needles constitute the darkest and most shade-tolerant foliage of the conifers.

CAUTION: *Yew seeds, twigs, and foliage are extremely poisonous to people and animals.*

HOW TO GROW

Yews are adapted to both sunny and deeply shaded sites in moderate and cold climates but do not thrive in the heat of the South. They require nearly neutral soil, preferring rich loam but adapting to sand or well-drained clay. Though long-lived in ideal conditions, yews are short-lived where drainage is poor. They need regular water to become established, then will endure brief periods of drought. Give them planting sites protected all year from reflected heat and, in winter, from direct sun and drying winds.

LANDSCAPE USE

Tall forms of yew are excellent for screening out unattractive views or as windscreens. Midsized and low forms are favored for foundation plants and hedges.

Top Choices

- *T. baccata* 'Adpressa', English yew, is a wide-spreading, dense shrub with short, dark green needles. It can be kept to a height of 4 to 5 feet with regular pruning. 'Adpressa Fowle' reaches 6 feet tall and spreads to 16 feet. Zones 6 to 8.

- *T. cuspidata,* Japanese yew, is a multi-stemmed shrub with dark needles. An excellent hedge plant, it can take any amount of pruning. Unpruned, it slowly reaches 40 feet. Japanese yew tolerates shade and urban pollution. Zones 4 to 7.

- *T.* x *media*, hybrid yew, comprises a diverse group ranging from low, spreading forms to tall, columnar forms. 'Hatfieldii' is a dark green pyramid that grows to 10 feet and retains a bright green color throughout winter. 'Runyan' reaches 4 feet high by 8 feet wide with graceful, slightly arching branches. 'Tauntonii' thrives in warmer regions and is immune to winter burn when grown in cold climates. Zones 4 to 8.

MAINTAINING SHAPE
WITH PRUNING

Many of the yews seen in modern landscapes are sheared into formal shapes. While shearing is an excellent way to maintain geometric shapes, pruning is preferred when a more relaxed appearance is desired.

Prune yews in summer when the spring growth has reached its full extent. Using hand pruners, clip off the more unruly branches that poke above the rest of the plant. Be sure to cut the branches where they join another stem so you don't leave behind stubby stumps.

Pruning requires less time than shearing. As a bonus, songbirds prefer pruned yews for shelter far more than sheared ones.

VIBURNUM
Viburnum

Zones: 3–9 (varies by species)

Type: Evergreen or deciduous

Light: Full sun to light shade

Size: Varies by species

Uses: Foundation planting, screen, shrub border, specimen

Interest: Fragrant flowers; colorful fall foliage and berries

In American landscapes, viburnums are the standard that all other shrubs must try to match. The numerous species of these diverse plants combine the best elements that shrubs have to offer, including: beautiful, fragrant blossoms; attractive foliage and berries; a neat, tidy form; and durability to heat and cold.

HOW TO GROW

Most viburnums prefer fertile, moist, well-drained soil in sun or light shade. Deciduous forms tend to do better in full sun, while the evergreens like part shade. They tolerate heavy soil and some alkalinity, preferring loam and acidic conditions. In the South, nematodes—small worms that attack the roots of plants—can be a problem. Control this pest by adding compost to the soil, which attracts organisms that prey on nematodes.

Planting marigolds and Madagascar periwinkle under or near the shrubs also helps.

LANDSCAPE USE

Most viburnums are midsized shrubs, especially useful as foundation plants or specimens, while others are useful as hedges, screens, or border plants. When in doubt about which shrub to choose for your landscape, a viburnum is probably the answer.

Top Choices

- *V.* x *burkwoodii*, Burkwood viburnum, has intensely fragrant blossoms. Semievergreen in mild climates, this 8- to 10-foot shrub is excellent in urban sites. 'Mohawk' is a stunning variety with deep red buds and clove-scented flowers. The lustrous green leaves turn vibrant shades of orange-red in fall. Zones 4 to 8.

- *V. carlesii*, Korean spice viburnum, has one of the sweetest fragrances of all shrubs. The spicy scent of 'Cayuga' is so sweet you might think it could double as dessert. The white flower clusters open from pinkish red buds in spring. 'Compactum' grows 3 feet tall, displaying dark green leaves and clusters of sweet, white flowers. Zones 4 to 7.

- *V. dilatatum* 'Erie', linden viburnum, is a prized accent plant that grows to 6 feet and spreads to 10 feet. Flat white flower clusters cloak the branches in spring and a striking display of long-lasting, coral-red fruits decorate them in fall and winter. The lustrous green foliage develops a bronze-burgundy fall color. Zones 5 to 7.

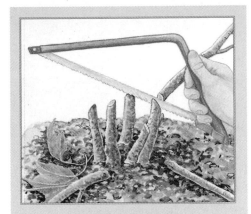

REJUVENATING
SHRUBS

Many shrubs that are overgrown, old, or long-neglected can be rejuvenated by severe pruning. This type of pruning should be done when the plants are dormant, preferably in mid- to late winter. Select a pair of long-handled loppers for thin-caliber stems or a bow saw for thicker ones.

1 Place the loppers or saw blade at a slight angle against the stem and make a clean cut 4 to 6 inches above the soil.

2 Alter the height of the pruning cuts as you proceed so the stubs are not all the same length, but are staggered instead.

3 Continue pruning until all the stems are cut.

CHASTE TREE
Vitex agnus-castus

Zones: 7–9

Type: Deciduous

Light: Full sun

Size: 10–20 ft. tall, 10–15 ft. wide

Uses: Shrub border, specimen

Interest: Upright lilac flowers; gray-green, aromatic foliage

Chaste tree has fragrant, 4- to 10-inch long, tapered spikes of lilac-purple flowers that stand up like candles from midsummer to fall when few other shrubs are in bloom. The blossoms are somewhat reminiscent of butterfly bush, long-lasting, and often used in dried arrangements. This ornamental, multi-stemmed shrub, sometimes called pepperbush, can be trained as a small tree. The soft, textured leaves are aromatic and release a peppery fragrance when crushed.

HOW TO GROW
Chaste tree tolerates a wide range of soils, growing well in dry and wet conditions and everything else in between. Its one requirement for heavy bloom is a long, hot summer. If faded blossoms are deadheaded promptly, the plants continue to flower into fall. Flower color is

less intense when plants are grown in rich, moist soils.

Keep chaste tree to a manageable size by cutting the stems to within 6 to 12 inches of the ground every two or three years. In Zone 6, chaste tree can be grown as an herbaceous perennial and cut to the ground in late winter or early spring. New shoots will emerge in spring and come quickly into bloom.

LANDSCAPE USE

With the lower branches removed, the attractive vase shape of chaste tree accents creeping ground covers or perennials clustered beneath it. Unpruned, it becomes a broad shrub, as impressive in bloom as it is a late-summer accent. Set chaste tree at the end of a border with spring-blooming shrubs, always giving it room to reach its full width. It is a wonderfully self-reliant shrub and, when left on its own, stays attractive for years with little maintenance.

Top Choices

- *V.* 'Alba' has the same habit as chaste tree and bears white flowers.

- *V.* 'Rosea' is slightly hardier than the species, surviving into the warmer regions of Zone 5. It produces pink blossoms.

- *V.* 'Silver Spire' bears white flowers on fast-growing stems.

Taylor's Tips

SPRING PRUNING

Because chaste tree is late to leaf out in spring, it is difficult to tell the extent of winter damage early in the season. Wait until growth is strong in spring before trimming dead twigs back to live wood. If damage is slight, trim lightly; if damage is heavy, cut the stems back to the ground.

SHOWING OFF

Chaste tree loves the limelight and should be placed where it will stand out as a cool complement to a green lawn or background fence. In spring and fall, the foliage provides a gray-green backdrop for roses and lavender and the pale gray foliage of artemisia.

If space allows, plant a second chaste tree with a contrasting bloom color.

WEIGELA
Weigela florida

Zones: 5–9

Type: Deciduous

Light: Full to part sun

Size: 10 ft. tall,
8 ft. wide

Uses: Mass planting,
foundation planting,
shrub border

Interest: Funnel-
shaped spring flowers

Weigela is famous for the abundant, voluptuous flowers that make up for its otherwise plain appearance and awkward profile. For several weeks in spring, this shrub flaunts countless pink to red, funnel-shaped blossoms on every stem in a showstopping performance. Viewed from a distance, it is a frothy, colorful mound. Up close, the individual blossoms reveal pale throats or contrasting stamens. Widely planted decades ago, this old-fashioned shrub is enjoying a comeback as new cultivars offer bright red flowers, bronze foliage, and compact size.

HOW TO GROW

Though weigela blossoms well in part sun, it sets the heaviest bloom in full sun. It grows best in loose, fertile soil, but it is easygoing enough to adapt to most growing conditions. It will grow in difficult urban sites and tolerates air pollution. To keep weigela shapely and diminish its rather rangy habit, cut some of the oldest stems to the ground each year after flowering. Remove any suckering growth, leaving only a few vigorous stems to increase the shrub's spread. To renew flowering wood, cut back branches that have bloomed to the next lower branch or cut back all stems back by half.

LANDSCAPE USE

Weigela blooms in prime time in spring, along with mock orange, late-flowering lilac, and spirea. Together they make a breathtaking display in a large garden. Tall weigelas can easily be mixed with any of these shrubs in a deep border. Weigelas that are cut back each year should be placed at the front of borders or associated with other low-growing plants.

Variegated Weigela

- W. 'Variegata' adds an especially gentle look to the garden. With pink flowers and foliage with creamy yellow leaf margins, it is a study in contrasts; the foliage adds visual texture to the garden. The plant spreads 6 to 10 feet wide and reaches 4 to 6 feet tall. 'Variegata' is a sturdy background plant that enhances deeper shades of green. It is a nice addition to a perennial border or an island bed with ground covers and spikes of iris foliage.

Taylor's Tips

OLD-FASHIONED PARTNERS

Cottage pink, also called border carnation, is an old-fashioned partner for weigela. Growing only 1 to 2 feet tall, the plants are covered with red, pink, or white blossoms that skirt the weigela throughout summer after its heavy bloom. Choose cottage pink in a color that coordinates with the weigela blossoms, since the shrub tends to bloom sporadically throughout summer and fall.

KEEPING A LOW PROFILE

The soft pink or red blossoms of this old-fashioned shrub seem to call out for a white picket fence, but its irregular shape when out of blossom does not suit it for a high-profile location.

Several of its compact cultivars, however, are perfectly suitable at garden entries. 'Lucifer', 'Minuet', 'Rumba', 'Samba', and 'Tango' are all red-flowering and under 3 feet tall, some with tinted foliage.

Extra-cold-hardy compact weigelas include 'Minuet' and 'Vanicek', also red, and pink 'Polka', hardy to Zone 4.

GLOSSARY

Acidic soil: Soil with a pH less than 7, common in areas with high rainfall.

Acid reacting: Substance, usually fertilizer, that when added to the soil, increases acidity and lowers pH. Fertilizers formulated for hollies, camellias, and rhododendrons are acid reacting.

Alkaline soil: Soil with a pH above 7, common in climates with low rainfall.

Bonsai: The art of creating a dwarf-sized tree or shrub by training; creates a miniature plant that conveys the illusion of great age.

Cane: Long, thin, flowering woody stem that rises directly from the ground.

Catkin: Dense and slender, often drooping, spike of flowers lacking petals; either male or female, as on birch trees.

Chlorosis: Yellowing of leaves caused by iron deficiency; often due to soil alkalinity preventing the uptake of iron.

Coniferous: Having cones, usually evergreen with needlelike foliage.

Creeping: Having prostrate stems that spread along the soil surface and root as they grow.

Crown: The part of the plant at or near the soil line where the upright stem(s) meets the below-ground roots.

Cultivar: A cultivated variety produced through vegetative propagation or cloning.

Deadheading: Removing faded flowers during the growing season to stimulate the development of new flowers and prevent seed formation.

Deciduous: Having leaves that drop off at one time each year; not evergreen.

Double flower: A flower with a greater number of petals than normal, giving it a full appearance.

Dwarf: Plant genetically identical to its species but shorter and often slow-growing.

Espalier: Plant with branches trained to grow in a flat pattern against a wall or other support.

Evergreen: Woody plant that does not drop all of its leaves in the same season.

Genus: Category of plants of closely related species.

Herbaceous: Nonwoody plants that die to the ground each year.

Hip: The usually round and highly colored fruit of a rose; contains seeds.

Humus: Organic matter in the soil derived from the decomposition of animal and vegetable remains.

Hybrid: Plant resulting from a cross most often between two species or varieties.

Layering: Propagation by securing a stem to the ground, then partially covering it with soil to promote root formation while still attached to the parent plant.

Leaf mold: Partially decomposed leaves used as mulch or humus.

Lime: Soil amendment containing calcium used to raise soil pH to reduce acidity and increase alkalinity; some forms also contain magnesium.

Loam: A natural blend of clay, silt, and sand rich in organic matter.

Mulch: Protective material spread over the soil for one or more of the following purposes: to control weeds, conserve moisture, protect plant roots, moderate soil temperature, or prevent erosion.

Neutral: Soil with a pH of 7, neither acidic nor alkaline.

Node: That part of a stem where buds, leaves, or branches are attached.

Organic matter: Plant material in various stages of decomposition.

Panicle: Multi-branched flower cluster that blooms from bottom to top.

pH: An expression of the hydrogen ion content of soil; it measures the soil's relative acidity or alkalinity.

Rhizome: Underground stem—often long, slender, and horizontal—with nodes from which new upright shoots may grow.

Runner: Slender shoot or stem lying under or on the ground, able to root at the tip or along its nodes.

Shrub: Woody perennial, usually multi-stemmed from the ground level or near it, and smaller than a tree.

Single flower: A flower possessing the minimum number of petals for its kind, usually four, five, or six.

Species: Group of closely related individuals that can breed together and produce similar offspring.

Specimen: A single, prominently placed plant with highly valued ornamental features.

Spike: Single-stemmed flower cluster in which each flower lacks a stalk.

Spreading: Growing laterally or horizontally by elongation of branches from the main stem.

Stamen: The male, pollen-bearing part of a flower, often long, slender, and in groups in the center of a flower.

Standard: Plant not normally grown as a tree that is trained into a tree form with a single stem topped by a ball of foliage.

Stolon: Horizontal, aboveground stem, often long and slender, with nodes from which new upright shoots may grow.

Sucker: Shoot arising from underground, usually from roots and often from grafted rootstock.

Tomentose: Characterized by a soft, woolly coating of hairs.

Topiary: A plant that has been pruned to a new shape, forming a living sculpture.

Variegated: Marked with stripes, blotches, or some regular or irregular pattern of color other than green.

Variety: Subdivision of a species consistently showing differences throughout generations.

Vegetative propagation: Production of a new plant through cloning and not from seed; methods include layering, cutting, dividing, and grafting.

Zone Map

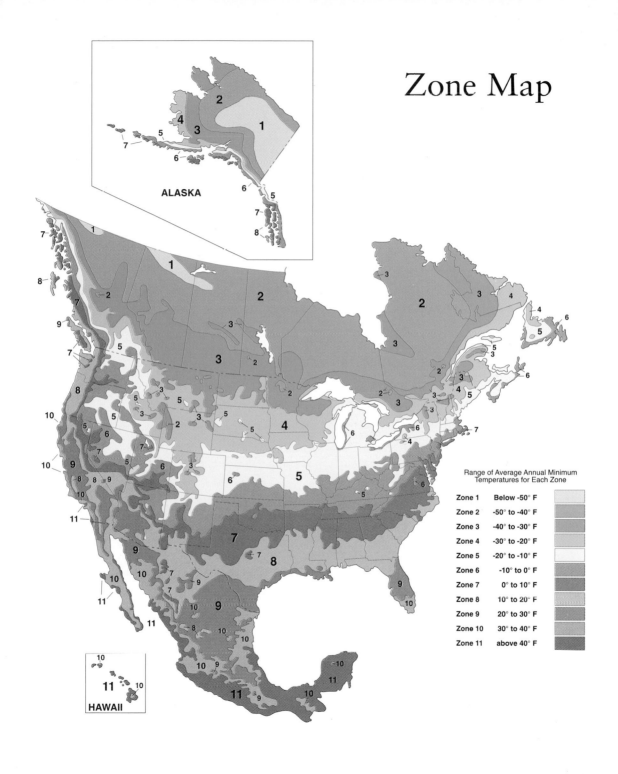

ALASKA

HAWAII

Range of Average Annual Minimum
Temperatures for Each Zone

Zone 1	Below -50° F	
Zone 2	-50° to -40° F	
Zone 3	-40° to -30° F	
Zone 4	-30° to -20° F	
Zone 5	-20° to -10° F	
Zone 6	-10° to 0° F	
Zone 7	0° to 10° F	
Zone 8	10° to 20° F	
Zone 9	20° to 30° F	
Zone 10	30° to 40° F	
Zone 11	above 40° F	

PHOTOGRAPHY & ILLUSTRATION CREDITS

David Cavagnaro
104

Christine L. Dupuis
13

Chuck and Barbara Crandall,
Crandall & Crandall
88, 106, and 114

Derek Fell
Front Cover, 10, 22, 34, 40, 48,
60, 74, 100, 108, and 112

Bill Johnson
36

Beverly Duncan, illustrator
11, 21, 29, 33, 45, 47, 51, 59, 67,
75, 87, 95, 99, 109, and 111

Marla Murphy
78

Jerry Pavia,
Jerry Pavia Photography, Inc.
Title Page, 12, 14, 20, 24, 39, 42,
44, 46, 58, 62, 66, 76, 82, 90, 96,
and 98

Richard Shiell
16, 18, 26, 28, 38, 50, 56, 68, 70,
72, 80, 86, 92, 94, 102, and 110

Steven M. Still
8 and 32

Joseph G. Strauch Jr.
52, 54, and 84

White Flower Farm, Inc.
30 and 64

INDEX

Storey Communications, Inc.
Pownal, Vermont

President: M. John Storey
Executive Vice President: Martha M. Storey
Chief Operating Officer: Dan Reynolds
Director of Custom Publishing: Deirdre Lynch
Project Manager: Barbara Weiland
Author: Rosemary McCreary
Book Design: Betty Kodela
Design Assistance: Jen Rork
Horticultural Review: Charles W. G. Smith